Cross in Tensions

Princeton Theological Monograph Series

K. C. Hanson, Charles M. Collier, and
D. Christopher Spinks, Series Editors

Recent volumes in the series

Kevin Twain Lowery
Salvaging Wesley's Agenda: A New Paradigm for Wesleyan Virtue Ethics

Matthew J. Marohl
Faithfulness and the Purpose of Hebrews: A Social Identity Approach

D. Seiple and Frederick W. Weidmann, editors
*Enigmas and Powers: Engaging the Work of Walter Wink
for Classroom, Church, and World*

Stanley D. Walters
Go Figure!: Figuration in Biblical Interpretation

Paul S. Chung
Martin Luther and Buddhism: Aesthetics of Suffering, Second Edition

Ralph M. Wiltgen
*The Founding of the Roman Catholic Church in Melanesia
and Micronesia, 1850–1875*

Steven B. Sherman
*Revitalizing Theological Epistemology: Holistic Evangelical
Approaches to the Knowledge of God*

David Hein
Geoffrey Fisher: Archbishop of Canterbury, 1945–1961

Mary Clark Moschella
*Living Devotions: Reflections on Immigration, Identity,
and Religious Imagination*

Cross in Tensions

Luther's Theology of the Cross as Theologico-Social Critique

PHILIP RUGE-JONES

PICKWICK *Publications* · Eugene, Oregon

CROSS IN TENSIONS
Luther's Theology of the Cross as Theologico-Social Critique

Princeton Theological Monograph Series 91

www.wipfandstock.com

ISBN 13: 978-1-55635-522-6

Cataloging-in-Publication data:

Ruge-Jones, Philip.

    Cross in tensions : Luther's theology of the cross as theologico-social critique /
Philip Ruge-Jones.

    Eugene, Ore.: Pickwick Publications, 2008

    xvi + 204 p.; 23 cm. — Princeton Theological Monograph Series 91
Includes bibliographical references.

    Includes a translation of Lucas Cranach's *The Passion of the Christ and of the
Antichrist* by Keith Killinger.

    ISBN 13: 978-1-55635-522-6

    1. Luther, Martin, 1483–1546—theology. 2. Jesus Christ—Crucifixion—
theology. I. Cranach, Lucas, 1472—1553. II. Killinger, Keith. III. Title. IV. Series.

BR332.5 .R86 2008

Dedicated to
my Doctoral Father
Vítor Westhelle
Theologian of the Cross

Contents

Illustrations

Lucas Cranach, Passion of Christ and of the Anti-Christ

Images provided by the Kessler Reformation Collection of the Pitts
    Theology Library

Acknowledgments

As the final pages of this book are written I am filled with a deep sense of thankfulness to the many people who have made this work possible. First of all, I would like to thank my whole family and especially my wife, Lori, without whom this would never have happened. She has provided support of every kind throughout the several years that I have been working toward this goal. She is a faithful companion whom I dearly love. Our children, Luisa and Luke, have grown with this book. One was born right before the research began and the other followed soon afterward. Their long naps made this writing possible.

Many communities of faith have journeyed with me during this time and I remember them with gratitude. I think especially of San Pedro (Coronel, Chile), Resurrección (Hempstead, New York), Central Lutheran (Edgerton, Wisconsin), First Lutheran (Janesville, Wisconsin), St. John's/San Juan (Austin, Texas), Lutheran Church of the Resurrection (Wimberley, Texas) and Living Word (Buda, Texas). In all of these I served among faithful people trying to discern the presence of the crucified Christ in our world.

As far as the specific work that led to this book, I recall the wonderful teachers with whom I had the pleasure of learning at the Lutheran School of Theology in Chicago. I came there wanting to study the theology of the cross and found myself assigned to an amazing theologian from Brazil named Vítor Westhelle. He modeled for me the life of a theologian of the cross who is committed to the marginalized people of the world, but also passionately committed to academic excellence. He clarified and elevated the quality of my own work, and, I hope, of my own discipleship in the way of Christ. This book is dedicated to him. I also am thankful for the gifted teacher of Martin Luther and his theology, Kurt Hendel. He showed me much about the reformer that I had not seen by drawing me deeper into the primary texts. He helped me pursue my own insights even when they went in directions that he would not choose to take. I also think of Philip Hefner with whom I read the Canadian theologian of the cross Douglas John Hall in my first year of doctoral study. He challenged me to see the larger world beyond my own idiosyncratic worldview and then demonstrated in his own theological vocation a willingness to ardently pursue areas previously unknown to him. If Dr. Hefner drew me into Hall, José David Rodríguez led me through the world of Spanish-speaking theologians of the cross. He demonstrated to me a vibrant love for lively conversations about *el sabor de la vida*. In addition to these fine theologians, others have provided institutional support without which this work could not have occurred. High praise is due to Irene Connors who kept me in good standing with the seminary through her wise guiding and persistent sense of what the right thing to do would be. She is a gift to our doctoral program. Also, very supportive of my endeavors have been the directors of doctoral studies, Wes Fuerst and Mark Thomsen. I thank them for all they have done.

In addition to the staff and faculty of LSTC, the students made learning a pleasure. I thank our weekly seminar group from Jimmy's, especially Elaine Siemsen and Caryn Riswold, who have walked the long walk with me. Many international students with whom I studied also broadened my vision of life. I especially am thankful for my friend, Kwong Sang Li, with whom I shared many conversations about Luther and ministry, and Andrea Ng'weshemi, who is a wonderful global theologian and pastor.

My good fortune continued as I served for a year as an instructor at the Lutheran Seminary Program in the Southwest. To my amazement I was paid to do what I most love: read books, lead conversations with engaging students, and think about God. I have had the pleasure of working with the skilled leadership of Augie Wenzel who was there with enthusiasm for myself and my family since day one. I also have had the pleasure of many profound, soulful conversations with biblical scholar and friend, Ray Pickett. He provided much sage advice as my family has sought to discern where God is leading us next. Also to Trish Karli, to Jacquelyn Allen [font of all Austin information], and to Lucille Hager (RIP), who had overseen the creation of a very fine theological library, I owe them many thanks.

The final form of this book came together during my time at Texas Lutheran University. My colleagues there are deeply treasured. Norman Beck, Carolyn Schneider, David Baer, Mark Gilbertson, and Daryl

Koenig (RIP) have been highly supportive of my work. A section of this work was read with invaluable comments from Carolyn Austin's Works in Progress group at Texas Lutheran University. Many other friends at TLU make it a place at which I truly enjoy serving. Texas Lutheran also supplied me with a semester of sabbatical during which this book found its final form.

My editor Charlie Collier was enthusiastic from the beginning of our work together. I was very excited that he encouraged me to include the pamphlet at the end of this book. The pamphlet came together due to the generosity of many people. Thanks to Patrick Graham and Margaret Peddle of the Pitts Theology Library of Chandler School of Theology. They provided me with wonderful images the Kessler Reformation Collection. My provost, John Masterson, and dean, John Sieben both provided needed financial support for this project. And finally Keith Killinger did intensive language work to provide the excellent translation that you will read of the pamphlet. God has blessed me with so many good people in my life; all praise and honor be God's!

Introduction

THE QUESTIONS THAT THIS BOOK RAISES AS WELL AS THE RESPONSES
it begins to formulate reflect the itinerary of its author. I was raised in
a Lutheran parsonage in the Midwest of the United States in a community where, for the most part, people were of European descent. I am
conscious that I was born into a power-laden place within the whole
web of the world community. I state this at the beginning, not in order to get it out of the way, but that the reader might keep it in sight.
Questions about how my location and experience might be biasing, or,
for that matter, enriching my perspective are welcomed.

I was raised in a Lutheran family.[1] My mother is a life long Lutheran
who lived out the unconditional love that she had learned from the
story of Jesus. She lives graciously in the knowledge of a gracious God.
So firm was her lived testimony that my father upon meeting her came
back to the Christian church after a long absence. He soon went to college in order later to go to seminary. A Lutheran by conversion, his own
witness was decisively shaped by his understanding of the God who
justifies sinners. Having imbibed from this grace oriented faith from
my childhood on, I later had the opportunity to discern its meaning
in a more rigorously academic way at Luther Seminary in St. Paul,
Minnesota, and later at the Lutheran School of Theology at Chicago.
All of this by way of recognizing that my present struggling with Luther
should be of no surprise; he is one of the those who has been present
with me wherever I have gone.

In August of 1987, I left the United States for an internship in Chile.
For two years I lived and learned in the Lutheran church, San Pedro,
located a few blocks from the ocean. More than a decade before my arrival my own country helped Pinochet destabilize and overthrown the
democratically-elected president, Salvador Allende. All of the people I

---

1. A book I have written directed toward a popular audience chronicles and interprets theologically the various phases of my life discussed in this introduction. See *The Word of the Cross in a World of Glory*.

met in Chile had lost loved ones in the reign of terror that the United States government had backed. Yet these people witnessed to the God of life who was with them even in death. As I thought about going back to the United States, I found that my Chilean experience called me to struggle anew with the reformer. Martin Luther, his thought and life, was what met me by the water's end in the hazy light before dawn. He came to wrestle with me as I looked at my return home. In such dim light, it has not always clear if I am wrestling with a demon—I recall Luther's words against the peasants, "smite, stab, and kill"—or with a messenger of God—"true theology is in the crucified Christ." Some warn me to just let him go, and move on; allowing him to touch me too deeply might cause my theology to limp along, they warn. And yet I wrestle on, hopeful that the struggle will indeed yield a blessing. I am encouraged by others along the way who have found in Luther's theology of the cross godly wisdom to confront the powerful and lift up the lowly.

Just as God has continued to call me to struggle with Luther, God has lead me to places where I do that in the midst of people who hear God's voice in the languages of South America. After seminary I worked at a church in New York that was primarily made up of people from El Salvador, Ecuador, and the Dominican Republic. For four years, we sought to discern together God's call to faithfulness. The doctoral studies that first cultivated this present work were guided under the commitment and wisdom of Vítor Westhelle, a Brazilian theologian. As I finish this book I live in Texas and am surrounded by Mexican Americans and others who enrich my life immensely and who provide me with fresh perspectives from which to think about Luther.

The issues raised in my own journey, I have come to believe, reflect a struggle within many of my generation. A whole generation of Luther scholars, for example, are beginning to look at Luther in his full historic embeddedness. They are asking about the mutual influences of Reformation movements and the political, social, economic and cultural world of the time. This quest within Luther studies is indicative of a broader movement. Among many of us a hunger is awakening that longs to speak of God in a way that does not lift us out of our historical, social, and political lives, but that draws us deeper into them. We are weary of a god divorced from history or historic reality drained of spirit. We long to relate holistically to the holy God revealed in Jesus

Christ. This study on the theology of the cross hopes to be one small contribution in that quest.

Thus, the purpose of this book is to examine the way that Luther's theology of the cross interacted with his own existential, political, economic, religious and social context. Within Luther's own world, his theology of the cross acted as a tool for radical social critique. His theology of the cross addressed not only the internal experience of the despairing individual, but also inserted itself in history in the midst of public, institutional struggles. In concrete social conflicts, Martin Luther, theologian of the cross, did not generically place all people on the same level before God, but rather took sides and attempted to reconfigure power relationships in favor of the marginalized. Those of us today who wish to place themselves faithfully in this movement must do likewise.

The book will begin with the work of prior interpreters of Luther's theology of the cross. I have proposed three models that these interpretations have presented for interpreting the theology of the cross. A diversity of perspectives is already present in the guild. Each approach brings gifts, but also shortcomings. After expounding the basic models, I ask if we might move further in understanding the social and political functioning of Luther's theology.

The second chapter will begin the task of a contextual interpretation of the theology of the cross. Utilizing contemporary research on the sixteenth-century context, a general map of the various power relationships—political, social, economic, ideological and religious—within which the theology of the cross was formed and performed will be suggested.

With this mapping of the context in mind, the next several chapters will articulate the theology of the cross as it arose in the early writings of Luther. Various texts will help us to articulate the contextual contours of Luther's early theology of the cross and the way that it opened up transformative possibilities for the faithful who were poor and marginalized. We also will raise the question of the social functioning of Luther's theology as the Reformation movement took decisive turns in its orientation toward establishing its own legitimacy. My hope is that theologians of the cross today might find wisdom for the work ahead of us so that the church might be reformed and the world transformed.

Abbreviations

LW   Luther's Works (American Edition)

WA   Luthers Werke: Kritische Gesamtausgabe

WA BR   Luthers Werke: Kritische Gesamtausgabe, Briefwechsel

WA TR   Luthers Werke: Kritische Gesamtausgabe, Tischreden

1

Interpretations of Luther's Theology of the Cross

WHAT HAVE GREAT INTERPRETERS OF LUTHER'S THEOLOGY OF THE cross understood by his project? What themes unite them? What divides them? In what way do they take into account the complex power dynamics of the sixteenth century? I have divided the six theologians to be examined into three models: crisis or conflictive interpretations, proclamation interpretations, and mystical or sacramental interpretations. I recognize that distinctions are never as clear cut as models seem to imply; yet models do alert us to broad, important options in interpretation and are useful in this sense.

Crisis or Conflictive Theology of the Cross

Loewenich

In the height of the Luther Renaissance that began the last century, Walther von Loewenich offered a fresh and appreciative study called *Luther's Theology of the Cross*. While others had preceded him in examining this concern, he offered the first sustained and appreciative attempt at understanding Luther's theology of the cross within the whole corpus of the reformer's theological writings.[1] Loewenich breaks with prior interpreters in two ways. First, he sees the theology of the cross as the decisive element in all of Luther's theology. Thus he attempts to formulate the positive relationship between, for example, the use of the "Hidden God" in the relatively early *Heidelberg Disputation*, Luther's mid-career *Bondage of the Will*, and the later *Lectures on Genesis*. He argues that what on the surface appear to be contradictions can in fact

---

1. Loewenich, *Luther's Theology of the Cross*.

be harmonized. Yet by the fourth edition of this book, he expresses res-
ervations about the harmoniousness he had seen.[2]

Secondly, Loewenich appreciates the theology of the cross and is
unwilling to view it as an unfortunate, medieval, monkish remnant as
prior interpreters had. He understands the theology of the cross as more
than a point of historical debate; it becomes a contributing resource
in contemporary theological construction. This new appreciation occurs within the crisis of Post-World War I Germany. Karl Barth, Emil
Brunner, Eduard Thurneysen, and other crisis theologians felt disillu-
sionment at the support that their liberal teachers gave to the German
government's war policies. In light of this crisis, they pursued a new
direction for theological activity. God is the great negation of all human
assertions. Humanity stands in a perpetual state of crisis before God.
Yet, these theologians' generic critique of humanity also represented
a conflict between alternative human communities of discourse. The
concept of God's universal negation pitted the theologians of crisis
against their liberal teachers. The conflict that they identified was not
only between God and humanity, but also between certain humans who
glimpsed God faithfully and others who had betrayed the God revealed
in Jesus Christ. Their critique profoundly shifted power relationships
in twentieth-century theology. Older great lights grew dim as a space
opened for others to shine.

Loewenich's interpretation of Luther chants along with the protest
of the crisis theologians at several points. He rejects Schleiermacher's
liberal program for theological discourse. He turns from all that smacks
of mysticism with its turn inward. He offers a virulent criticism of
ecclesial infatuations with "theologies of glory."[3] He renders a universal
judgment on humanity and its religious pretensions. Loewenich clearly
marks the limits of human reason. Over and against all such arrogance,
he declares with the crisis theologians the power of the word and the
freedom of God.

Loewenich's own involvement in this conflict with the liberal
theologians and their ecclesial pretensions opened him to see parallel elements in Luther's theological context. The starting point of this
interpretation is the recognition that Luther's theology of the cross

2. Ibid., 221.
3. Ibid., 12, 18.

was forged in the midst of a public struggle with the church of his day. Having experienced the betrayal of God's mission within his own church, Loewenich will not miss the decisive role that Luther's ecclesiastical struggle played in shaping his theology. Luther's theology was forged in its combat "against a church that has become secure and smug."[4] That church had lost its divine direction. Loewenich recalls Luther's accusation:

> Truly, this wisdom of the cross and this new meaning of things is not merely unheard of, but is by far the most fearful thing even for the rulers of the church. Yet it is no wonder, since they have abandoned the Holy Scriptures and have begun to read unholy writings of men and the dissertations on finances instead.[5]

Both in the introduction to the book, and in the last pages of the second part, this theme frames Loewenich's interpretation. The theology of the cross functions "in a critical way against the papacy."[6] Loewenich writes:

> We dare never forget that Luther's theology of the cross cannot be dismissed as the brooding product of a lonely monk, but it proved its worth for him when he stepped forth into an unprecedented battle. Luther practiced this theology in the face of death. Here every sentence is soaked with his heart's blood. If anywhere, then in Luther's theology of the cross "doctrine and life" are in agreement.[7]

The "we" that begins this quotation is not incidental, and certainly does not refer solely to Luther interpreters. The warning is to the church of Loewenich's day. "Are we not today experiencing a return from a theology of glory to a theology of the cross similar to the one we observe in Luther? Hence our work is motivated by a living concern."[8] Even more specifically, the "we" is directed to Lutherans who have formally affirmed the theology of the cross, but denied it in their living.

> While the Lutheran church has clung faithfully to the "for the sake of Christ" (*propter Christum*) it surrendered Luther's theol-

4. Ibid., 12.
5. Ibid., 22.
6. Ibid., 128.
7. Ibid., 113.
8. Ibid., 14.

ogy of the cross all too quickly. The theology of glory that Luther opposed has made a triumphal entry also into his church. One occasionally wonders whether the doctrine concerning the cross has not even been forced to pay tribute to this theology of glory.[9]

This focus on the theology of the cross as forged in public combat has particular implications for the way that Loewenich chooses documents for study. The texts he sees as most important were written at the time when the Reformation became a public event. Thus the *Heidelberg Disputation*, written in 1518, is the necessary starting point for understanding the theology of the cross.[10] This "basic document of the theology of the cross,"[11] along with others of that period such as *operationes in psalmos* of 1519 to 1521,

> is the work of a man who suddenly finds himself removed from the quiet monastery and placed into battle with the world and must daily be prepared for martyrdom. He is doing theology in the face of death. All props that do not stand firm in the presence of the ultimate have been dropped.[12]

Because of this commitment to the public battle, Loewenich is uninterested in tracing the theology of the cross back to Luther's experience as a monk; while he does incorporate later writings, he always understands them as further developments of the central insights of the earlier, conflictive period.

Loewenich proclaims with utmost clarity that the theology of the cross is first and foremost an *epistemological* claim. Over and over again he states this; ". . . in Luther's theology of the cross we are not dealing with paraphrases of the monkish ideal of humility, but with a distinctive principle of theological knowledge. . . ."[13] The theology of the cross "has its place not only in the doctrine of the vicarious atonement, but it constitutes an integrating element for all Christian knowledge."[14] "What is

9. Ibid., 18.
10. Ibid., 171.
11. Ibid., 30.
12. Ibid., 82.
13. Ibid., 13.
14. Ibid., 17, 18.

involved here is the question about knowledge of God."[15] "The theology of the cross rejects speculation as a way to knowledge.... If the cross becomes the foundation of Christian thought, a theology of the cross results. For the cross cannot be disposed of in an upper story of the structure of thought."[16] The theology of the cross "involved the question of theological method, not just a practical-ethical question."[17] He chastises one interpreter because he "does not speak of the significance of the cross for knowledge, criticism and theology."[18] And finally, when Loewenich had reached the end of his work, he summarized his project in this way: "The goal of my investigation was to show that the theology of the cross was a theological principle of knowledge for Luther."[19]

What then was the shape of this knowledge? Loewenich builds upon theses nineteen and twenty of the *Heidelberg Disputation*, which are decisive for Luther's understanding. They read:

> That person does not deserve to be called a theologian who looks upon the invisible things of God as though they were clearly perceptible in those things which have actually happened. He deserves to be called a theologian, however, who comprehends the visible and manifest things of God seen through suffering and the cross.[20]

Loewenich summarizes the aspects of Luther's theology of the cross in five points. He states:

1. The theology of the cross as a theology of revelation stands in sharp antithesis to speculation.

2. God's revelation is an indirect, concealed revelation.

3. Hence God's revelation is recognized not in works but in suffering, and the double meaning of these terms is to be noted.

4. This knowledge of God who is hidden in his revelation is a matter of faith.

15. Ibid., 16.

16. Ibid., 27.

17. Ibid., 169 n. 2.

18. Ibid., 173 n. 2.

19. Ibid., 219.

20. Cited in ibid., 18, from LW 31.40. There are some problems with this translation that I will address at a later point in the dissertation.

5. The manner in which God is known is reflected in the practical thought of suffering.[21]

Questions of epistemology run through all of these aspects. The last four aspects clarify the first claim about knowing through revelation rather than speculation. What does Loewenich mean by each of these points?

First of all, the theology of the cross is a theology of revelation. As such, it stands against every human attempt to speculate about the nature of God on the basis of creation or reason. Over and against the scholastic theologians of his day, Luther asserts that metaphysical speculation does not lead to knowledge of God, but rather blinds us to God's presence as it was radically revealed in the cross of Christ. God is most clearly known in the cross of Christ, that event where all "Christian thinking must come to a halt."[22] This knowledge of God flies in the face of all human attempts to understand God; "The cross makes demands on Christian thought—demands which must either be acted on or ignored."[23] While the scholastic theologians try to define God in terms of their own church's quest for satisfaction, that is, in terms of power and might, God chooses to be revealed in the cross of Christ in terms of lowliness and weakness.

Thus, this revelation is hidden or concealed. God reveals Godself by hiding in what appears to speculation to be the very opposite of God. This brings Loewenich to Luther's understanding of the hidden God. Loewenich recognizes that this doctrine undergoes evolution throughout Luther's career, but he sees the decisive key to understanding its central insights in the *Heidelberg Disputation*. Knowledge of God should be available in the created order, but due to human sin, we cannot see it, but rather abuse the knowledge. God is hidden by our blindness. This, however, is not the final word, for "God wants to be known, his being seeks revelation."[24] This is the key to Luther's doctrine of God including the notion of hiddenness. Because of the abuse of creational knowledge of God, God must be revealed in a concealed manner. But this concealment is *for the sake of revelation.* This concealed revelation

21. Loewenich, *Luther's Theology of the Cross*, 22.
22. Ibid., 27.
23. Ibid., 27.
24. Ibid., 28.

takes place in that one place where human beings would not think to look for the reality of God: in the cross. How odd! For the *Disputation* makes clear what is visible in the cross where there is "nothing else to be seen than disgrace, poverty, death and everything that is shown us in the suffering Christ."[25] Who would look for God in this wasteland of poverty? Yet, precisely under the form of suffering God wills to reveal Godself. Loewenich follows Luther in calling attention to this revelation on Golgotha, but also in contemporary "sufferings" and "crosses." Thus Luther attacks the philosophically sophisticated epistemology employed by his rivals. The scholastic theologians confidently support the tyranny of the church with their abusive knowledge of God. Loewenich summarizes Luther's criticism of them in another document of this period:

> Just as the theology of glory prefers works to sufferings, glory to the cross, power to weakness, wisdom to foolishness, so philosophy would rather investigate the essences and actions of the creatures than listen to their groanings and expectations.[26]

Crucial to Luther's understanding in this period is that:

> The hidden God is none other than the revealed God. God is hidden for the sake of revelation. . . . The hidden God is none other than the crucified God. Who is a theologian of the cross? A theologian of the cross is one who speaks of the crucified and hidden God.[27]

This equation of hiddenness and revelation is an explicit rejection of interpretations of Luther that see hiddenness as the antithesis of revelation in his thought. Within this schema, hiddenness had been equated with the terrifying powerfulness of God in and of Godself. There God is an all-consuming, threatening reality. Loewenich argues that Luther is explicitly rejecting this concept in favor of God made known in suffering and crosses.

Having laid out this understanding of hiddenness, Loewenich moves toward that text that he believes might jeopardize his claim that the theology of the cross is present in all of Luther's work: *The Bondage of the Will*. This text has been appealed to by those interpreters of hiddenness whom Loewenich reproaches. Loewenich notes that Luther

25. *Disputation*, cited in Loewenich, *Luther's Theology of the Cross*, 28.

26. Loewenich, *Luther's Theology of the Cross*, 69.

27. Ibid., 30.

emphasizes the need for God to be revealed. God hidden from all sight offers no hope, but only condemnation. This God has chosen to become the preached, revealed, worshipped, clothed God for our sake. Note that the God who reveals Godself is none other than the same God who is normally hidden from us. The theme again is that "God must conceal himself in the word in order to be able to reveal himself. The revealed God is the clothed God."[28] A shift in terminology has taken place in relation to the meaning of hiddenness, but the dynamic that Luther indicated in the *Heidelberg Disputation* continues to dominate his discourse. What is more, the clothed God comes out on our behalf. "The revealed God is unconditional salvific will."[29] Yet Luther has more to say about God.

> While we are dealing with the revealed God we dare not forget about the hidden God. God has indeed revealed himself in his word, but God is greater than his word. God has not confined himself within the limits of the word. God's supreme attribute is his freedom.[30]

Here enters the problem. The hidden God might just override the "unconditional salvific will" of the revealed God. Hiddenness and revelation are no longer equated but may be diametrically opposed. "But can the unity of the godhead still be maintained under such conditions? . . . Has this not made revelation illusory?"[31] What happens to the certainty of salvation that the Christian had received?

Loewenich says that the key through this conceptual bog is in the role of faith. Faith knows that God exists beyond the revealed word, but does not seek God in that beyond. In fact, the experience of God's hiddenness from all sight is precisely the thing that calls for faith to cling to the God clothed in the word. Faith, by its very nature, is for Luther trust in what one cannot see. If we are to believe in God's goodness, then we must not be able to see it clearly or no faith would be required, but only sight. The same is true when the faithful confess their belief in the church. The church is not equated with that which holds itself before our eyes as church, but is a concealed and hidden reality inviting faith

28. Ibid., 33.
29. Ibid.
30. Ibid., 34.
31. Ibid.

in the unseen. Also the righteousness of God must be incomprehensible so as to require faith. Thus, argues Loewenich "we can conclude that if the revealed God is really to be present for faith, he must also be the hidden God. Consequently the revealed God would be none other than the hidden God."[32] A shift has taken place in the meaning of the hidden God. "In the former the idea of the hidden God means that revelation in principle is possible only in concealment; in the latter it means that also in the revealed God secrets remain. Both lines intersect in the concept of faith."[33]

We shall return to the importance of faith shortly. First we need to note the function of the hiddenness of God in *The Bondage of the Will*. The hidden God is a "warning against all too confident arguing with God's thoughts...."[34] It checks human assertions about their knowledge of God as well as their assertions about the faithfulness of the visible church. The hidden God introduces the element of tentativeness and risk into all human claims about God.

Loewenich finishes his survey of this concept with Luther's lectures on Isaiah (1527–1530). Many of the themes already discussed endure in these lectures: God is incomprehensible until "covered"; faith sees God where God is so deeply hidden as to appear nothing; the papacy trusts in its own great visible power. Yet the simultaneity of *hidden* and *revealed* give way to a dynamic of succession. The God who first seems hidden becomes visible for us through our perseverance in prayer and faith. Once again, Loewenich insists that the heart of Luther's theology of the cross is revelation. The question remained for Luther: how will we properly know God? The error of many interpreters is to lose this epistemological thrust and to drag Luther's understanding into the realm of metaphysics. In that case the continual tension and movement required by the faith that knows of God's broken presence is supplanted by "a rigid side-by-side relationship of two hypostases."[35] This error only occurs when the later emphasis on hiddenness as absence is not understood in relation to the more fundamental understanding of hiddenness in suffering as seen by the eyes of faith.

32. Ibid., 37.
33. Ibid., 38.
34. Ibid., 37.
35. Ibid., 44.

Faith is related to hiddenness, yet Luther has an even broader understanding of it. The eyes of faith look upon the cross and "a radical reversal of all existing orders of precedence and relationships take place."[36] The "crucified God . . . signifies the great *No* to reality."[37] As such, the crucifixion stands over and against human reason, understanding, and experience. Yet when faith clings to the cross, a whole new reason, understanding, and experience are the result for the believer. Faith equals understanding in the life of the Christian. Thus "[faith] is not only the negation of human possibility, but its realization as well."[38] We recall Luther's earlier contextual observation that philosophically driven scholastic theology was the epitome of human reason in his day. Yet it avoided human groanings and the cross in favor of glorious speculation. "One who has caught something of the wisdom of the cross knows that reason is a 'dangerous thing' (WA IX, 187, 5ff)."[39] But when faith clings to the cross it receives a whole new, wholly reversed reality.

Thus we come to Loewenich's final point. Knowledge of God hidden in suffering corresponds to the new life that is given for the faithful to live. The epistemology is to be embodied in "practical suffering." This suffering is summarized in four points:

1. Our life will be one of lowliness and disgrace.

2. Christ calls the Christian to a discipleship of suffering, trusting that it is in suffering that God meets us.

3. The "true meaning of Christ's suffering can be discovered only in the act of experiencing, acting, and suffering."

4. We are conformed to Christ as we experience the fact of the cross in our own lives.[40]

This brings Loewenich back full circle to Luther's critique of the church of his day and its way of knowing. The suffering of the Christian life exposes the falsity of the church of his day[41] that rejected the "treasure" of suffering that God offered to it. The church ignored the suffer-

36. Ibid., 50.
37. Ibid., 51.
38. Ibid., 64.
39. Ibid., 75.
40. Ibid., 118–23.
41. Ibid., 128.

ing of the neighbor, suffering that, more often than not, the church itself had inflicted upon him or her.

Loewenich has understood the theology of the cross in terms of its relationship to the conflict Luther had with the institutional church. Though Loewenich is helpful in this sense, does he goes far enough in mapping out the total conflictive context in which this thought takes place? Furthermore, is Loewenich right in his claim that Luther continues throughout his career to ask the same question in relation to the hidden God? Do not his shifts in the concept of the hidden God indicate shifts in broader commitments within Luther and his movement? Is it not the case that similar concepts came to function in very different ways as both the context and Luther's own commitments within it underwent a change?

Althaus

In 1926, three years before Loewenich's book was first published, Paul Althaus wrote an article titled "Die Bedeutung des Kreuzes im Denken Luthers."[42] The themes expressed in that paper have continued to be present in Althaus' whole lifetime of work. Resonances with Loewenich and his interpretation are quite clear in Althaus' career and at times Althaus' own relationship to Loewenich is explicitly mentioned. His best work on the theology of the cross that has been translated into English translation is found in *The Theology of Martin Luther*.[43]

Resonating with Loewenich's epistemological concern, Althaus locates the theology of the cross under the rubric of "The Knowledge of God: the Word of God and Faith." Althaus begins the section with a footnote marking his conversation with Loewenich for his particular understanding of the Luther's theology of the cross; this is rare in a book whose footnotes almost exclusively reference the reformer's own writing. Althaus also follows Loewenich in holding up theses 19 and 20 as the heart of the *Heidelberg Disputation*. These, again, define the theologian of the cross and the theologian of glory in contradistinction. The two kinds of theologians are marked by different epistemological priorities. The first is attentive to God's always paradoxical revelation in sufferings; the second is fixed on the "invisible things of God" or on

42. Althaus, "Die Bedeutung des Kreuzes im Denken Luthers," 97–107.

43. Althaus, *Theology of Martin Luther*, 25–35.

"works". Althaus echoes what Loewenich made clear in his third aspect of the theology of the cross when he asserts:

> Luther uses "works" not only in the sense of God's works but also in the sense of man's works; and "sufferings" refers not only to Christ's suffering but also to man's suffering. Luther makes the transition from the one to the other as though it were self-evident.[44]

This self-evident transition brings Althaus to a recognition of the link between epistemology and ethics. "For Luther, concern for the true knowledge of God and concern for the right ethical attitude are not separate and distinct but ultimately one and the same. The theology of glory and the theology of the cross each have implications for both [epistemology and ethics]."[45] Thus, Althaus introduces the effects of Luther's critique on the combined forces of the scholastic theologians' metaphysical speculation and the system of work righteousness orchestrated by their church:

> Natural theology and speculative metaphysics which seek to learn to know God from the works of creation are in the same category of the work righteousness of the moralist. Both are ways in which man exalts himself to the level of God. Thus both either lead men to pride or are already expressions of such pride. Both serve to "inflate" man's ego. Both use the same standard for God and for man's relationship to God: glory and power.[46]

Althaus sees this important link that Luther makes as central to his thought. "Luther recognizes the inner relationship and even the identity of religious intellectualism and moralism. He shows that both are in opposition to the cross. These are two of the deepest insights of his theology."[47] Over and against the scholastic or churchly quest for glory and power stand the hard cross of Christ and our crosses. Captive to this reality, we know:

> God meets us in death, in the death of Christ, but only when we experience Christ's death as our own death. The death of Christ leads us to an encounter with God only when it becomes our

44. Ibid., 26–27.
45. Ibid., 27.
46. Ibid.
47. Ibid., 28.

death. Contemplating the death of Christ necessarily becomes a
dying together with him.[48]

In this understanding, revelation is always hidden or concealed. The
confidence with which church officials point to a historical institution and
claim it as the empirical church only exposes their theology of glory. The
theology of the cross stands against all such claims to glory and power
achieved in God's name. Faith knows another way. "To believe means to
live in constant contradiction of empirical reality and to trust one's self
to that which is hidden."[49] No single breakthrough to reality occurs, but
rather a constant process of struggle between human criteria and God's
hidden revelation occurs again and again. "Faith thus stands in constant
conflict; and it comes to life only when it breaks through the reality accessible to reason."[50] Then it knows what is really real.

How does Althaus look at *The Bondage of the Will* in terms of the
theology of the cross? The relationship that an interpreter assumes toward this document often indicates structural keys to the larger picture
that he or she presents of Luther. Althaus sees Luther's concept of the
hidden God as taking a decisive turn by the time of *The Bondage of the
Will.* From the early days of the *Heidelberg Disputation*, "the concept
has a completely different meaning."[51] Luther moves beyond the appropriate concern of the Apostle Paul that God's freedom be respected.
Althaus claims that the concern for God's hidden will in the later Luther
threatens the graciousness of the promise known in Christ:

> this knowledge of the hidden God lies like a wide shadow across
> the picture of God's revealed will. In comparison to the Bible, a
> shift in emphasis has taken place. It is one thing not to hide the
> sobering fact that God also hardens men's hearts and in the fear
> of God, to take it seriously as the Bible does; it is, however, quite
> another thing to take—as Luther does—the mystery that con-
> fronts us in the history of God's dealing with men and with peo-
> ples, a mystery which certainly conflicts with God's will to save
> as we know it, and develop it into a full-blown doctrine of God's
> double will, of the duality and extensive opposition between the
> hidden and the revealed God. . . . We must ask whether Luther's

48. Ibid.
49. Ibid., 33.
50. Ibid.
51. Ibid., 277.

> doctrine of the hidden God as it is presented in *The Bondage of the Will* does not abrogate the rest of his theology as we have come to know it. . . . Is it not immeasurably dangerous, even deadly, to man's trust in the word of promise? It actually asserts that God, according to his secret will, to a great extent disagrees with his word offering grace to all men. [52]

Yet Althaus, though concerned about the systematic implications of this doctrine, does see its usefulness as a necessary part of proclamation. The concept of the bondage of the will safeguards the sovereignty of God against all human attempts at control. The divine assurance offered is always in danger of being converted into human boasting.

> Finally, we remind ourselves again that Luther declares that the hidden God and his secret activity must be discussed *for the sake of the elect!* In the final analysis, Luther does not establish a theoretical doctrine of double predestination as Calvin does. In spite of all appearances to the contrary, his theology is at this point completely untheoretical and pastoral. His idea of the hidden God, finally intends only to purify Christians' faith from all secret claims and all self-security by proclaiming the freedom of God's grace.[53]

While this warning against self-security is valid, in the end one wonders if Althaus has taken the importance of history seriously enough in his proposal. The attraction of Luther's theology of the cross to the people of his day was not merely its resourcefulness as a generic critique of human pretension. Rather, they were drawn to Luther's particular usage of this critique against the concrete pretensions of the church of his day. Moreover, the attraction to this critical function of the theology of the cross over and against the institutional church had to do with the complicity of the church in power dynamics that transcended strictly theological and ecclesial systems. The critique aimed at the church attacked not only its religious transgressions, but also the way its pretensions were concretely embodied in political, economic and social systems that robbed the people of life.

---

52. Ibid., 277–78.
53. Ibid., 286.

Proclamation Theology of the Cross

Ebeling

Gerhard Ebeling has not only written pervasively on the theology of the cross, but has also dominated current Luther scholarship in general to such an extent that he has set its paradigm. Within the area of Luther interpretation, Ebeling's ruts run deep, and many interpretative vehicles have traveled in the direction that he has established.

In his important book *Luther: An Introduction to his Thought*[54] Ebeling identifies the dynamics fundamental to Luther's thought. Ebeling argues that Luther is a university professor responsible for an impressive linguistic innovation. He was a teacher and preacher profoundly centered on a commitment to the word of God alone. Beginning with the struggles of his own conscience, not with ecclesial abuses, Luther developed a complex theology fraught with pairs of contradictory claims that are never synthesized, but always held in tension. Tensions between law and gospel, freedom and bondage, God hidden and God revealed pervade his reflections.

In each of these pairs, the two contradictory poles depend on and feed off of each other. Each is necessary for the other. Take law and gospel. Luther's concern is not that one swallow up the other, but that they be allowed to maintain their relationship of mutual tension and even hostility. The role of the theologian is to make proper distinctions between them so that we can understand the proper functioning of law and gospel in theology and the world. Making this proper distinction "is the touchstone of theology, the point which decides whether one has really grasped its true substance. . . ."[55] Ebeling states that the law always makes demands upon us, while the gospel always is promise or gift. In the tension between the human experience of having demands made upon one's conscience and the total graciousness of God's gift in Christ, the Christian is justified by God. Justification is the centerpiece of Luther's theology. It not only is the prince among other doctrines; it gives "a true significance to all other doctrines."[56] Justification occurs, when theology is properly understood, in a word-event.

---

54. See also Ebeling, "Die Definition des Menschen und seine Mortalität."
55. Ebeling, *Luther*, 111.
56. Ibid., 112.

> Christian preaching *is* the process in which the distinction be-
> tween the law and the gospel takes place. . . . the concern of
> Christian preaching is to put into practice the distinction be-
> tween the law and the gospel, that is, to carry on the progress
> of a battle, in which time and again the distinction between the
> law and the gospel is newly at issue and is made in practice. . . .
> But if the process of preaching is what it claims to be, that is, the
> process of salvation, then as the distinction is made between the
> law and the gospel, so the event of salvation takes place. And the
> confusion of the two is not a misfortune of little significance, a
> regrettable weakness, but is evil in the strict sense, the total op-
> posite of salvation."[57]

Notice that making this distinction brings salvation while failure to do
so flirts with damnation. The proclaimed word is existentially vital. It is
neither abstract nor disinterested reflection.

> The word is only apprehended as such in concrete terms when
> the relationship is understood between what it *says* and what it
> *effects*, that is, when it is understood as an active and effective
> word and so is not separated from the situation in which it is
> uttered and which is changed by the word, but is regarded as
> one with it.[58]

This effective word

> possesses the character of an event with the power to bring
> about an ultimate decision. It has the power in so far as it touch-
> es and strikes man at his most sensitive point, the very heart of
> his being, where the decision is made as to what his position
> should be ultimately, that is, in the sight of God. Luther calls this
> point the "conscience" . . . What he means [by conscience] is that
> man is ultimately a hearer, someone who is seized, claimed, and
> subject to judgment, and that for this reason his existential be-
> ing depends upon which word reaches and touches his inmost
> being.[59]

Those who have not been freed by the gospel are in bondage as they
listen to the demands of the law made upon their inmost being. But
the gospel comes through the word of grace, causing one to trust solely

57. Ibid., 117.
58. Ibid., 119.
59. Ibid., 119–20.

in a righteousness that is given from above and is not one's own. This righteousness is

> not the righteousness of works, but the righteousness of faith; not active righteousness, but passive righteousness, given as a gift; not our own righteousness, but a righteousness from outside ourselves, imputed to us and because of this never becoming our own possession, even when it is given to us. It is in the strictest sense righteousness accepted by faith. Thus the Christian is in himself and on the basis of his own powers a sinner; but at the same time, outside himself, on the basis of what God does, and in the sight of God in Christ, he is one who is righteous.[60]

The gospel trilogy is this for Ebeling. First, we have God hidden in Christ salvifically. Second, the word alone declares and effects our wholly external righteousness. And, finally, faith clings to the promise alone, renouncing all claims to intrinsic righteousness.

Ebeling has a different appraisal of the chief concept described in *The Bondage of the Will* than that of our two earlier theologians. If Loewenich and Althaus approached *The Bondage of the Will* from the perspective of Luther's earlier writing, Ebeling moves in the reverse order. For Ebeling *The Bondage of the Will* interprets and correctly unfolds the underdeveloped structure suggested or hidden in the earlier writings. Thus, in *The Bondage of the Will* the hiddenness of God as omnipotence is not vanquished by the hiddenness of God as concealment in suffering, but rather the two definitions are maintained in mutual tension and even hostility. The latter depends for its vitality and effectiveness upon the reality of the other.

The question remains if one can actually live within this tension without resolving it in one direction or the other. Especially dangerous to our purposes is the possibility of being left with the omnipotent God whose presence casts a long shadow over the comfort available in the God who is present, though hidden, in suffering and shame. With the loss of focus on God's hidden presence in suffering, the poor are also lost from sight or relegated once again to the margins of the conversation. It is amazing that one so concerned about the cutting nature of the word event is so inattentive to the particular way in which that word does cut. Ebeling writes passionately about a word event that is neither

60. Ibid., 122.

abstract nor disinterested, but he does so in a historically abstract and disinterested way. His concern with judgment is merely that it happens. He is attentive only to the abstract phenomenon of judgment; he shows no attentiveness to the content of the law. Human assertion and abusive quests for power are not understood in their historical embeddedness. What Vítor Westhelle expresses in relation to Lutherans is particularly appropriate as a critique of Ebeling. Westhelle correctly observes "that Lutherans are often too quick to talk *formally* about *simul iustus et peccator* and too slow to recognize the particular content of sin itself."[61]

This lack of attention to the particularity of the law's attack is not a fair reading of Luther. He is intensely specific about the way that abusive power, especially though not exclusively that of the church, has destroyed the life and well being of the people. For Luther, God's judgment is concrete; it challenges the way that the neighbor is abused or neglected. Yet in Ebeling, the neighbor does not appear until the end of the whole project of theology. Only in the final pages of Ebeling's book does he raise "the last question, that of *the place of our fellow-man in what is said of God*."[62] Yet Luther clearly does not leave the neighbor until his final chapter. Luther is grossly misread when the neighbor is bracketed out of the process until theology, for all intents and purposes, is over. For Luther, the neighbor whose suffering we create or ignore cannot be divorced from the working of law. God's judgment is never abstract, but confronts a person in particular ways. Moreover, when the law is stripped of content and context, so is the gospel that follows it.[63]

Forde

Gerhard Forde, even more than any of our other writers, has employed the nomenclature of the theology of the cross with brutal persistence throughout his writing. In both his historical and his constructive work, Forde dips into the well of Luther's theology of the cross. The focus here will be on what would become his final book, *On Being a Theologian of the Cross: Reflections on Luther's Heidelberg Disputation, 1518*.[64]

---

61. Westhelle, "Luther and Liberation," 51.

62. Ebeling, *Luther*, 265.

63. Westhelle, "Luther and Liberation," 52.

64. Forde, *On Being a Theologian of the Cross*.

In the introduction to this book, Forde expresses three reasons for this book that meditates on the key document of Luther's *theologia crucis*. First of all, when it comes to Luther's theology of the cross, "there isn't much of anything in English one can recommend enthusiastically to the ordinary reader."[65] He acknowledges the indispensable contribution of Loewenich's work, but believes "it is heavy going" for the beginner. Secondly, Forde writes this book because much of what passes for theology of the cross is only about sentimentalized victimization. Forde states:

> Jesus is spoken of as the one who "identifies with us in our suffering," or the one who "enters into solidarity with us" in our misery. "The suffering of God," or the "vulnerability of God," and such platitudes become the stock-in-trade of preachers and theologians who want to stroke the psyche of today's religionists. But this results in rather blatant and suffocating sentimentality. God is supposed to be more attractive to us because he identifies with us in our pain and suffering. "Misery loves company" becomes the unspoken motif of such theology.[66]

This is not what Forde has in mind. This brings him to his third point. The theology of the cross can easily slip into a theology of glory with minimal, though immensely significant, shifts in the language employed. Forde wishes to learn Luther's language precisely so as to "hold the language in place."[67] Forde will stick close to the *Heidelberg Disputation*, which he carefully notes not only describes the practice of being a theologian of the cross, but "itself is the doing of a theologian of the cross."[68] This means:

> The Disputation itself, one might say, illustrates the manner in which theologians of the cross operate. Claimed, that is to say, killed and made alive by the cross alone as *the* story, theologians of the cross attack the way of glory, the way of law, human works, and free will, because the way of glory simply operates as a defense mechanism against the cross.[69]

65. Ibid., vii.
66. Ibid., viii.
67. Ibid., xi.
68. Ibid., xii.
69. Ibid., 12.

Forde's approach could also be seen as a kind of crisis theology of the cross, but it would have to carry a different sense than that which we applied to Loewenich and even Althaus. The conflict he alerts us to is not intrahuman; the crisis is a perpetual crisis of human beings in the presence of God Almighty. The crisis comes when "we in turn *suffer* the absolute and unconditional working of God upon us."[70] While Forde will have epistemological interest—he will ask about how we know God and what we must know about God—this epistemological interest is saturated with soteriology. To be a theologian of the cross means to be saved. Or, stated precisely, "the cross *is* the theo-logy."[71] The cross is God's word as an attack on all human pretensions of righteousness in the presence of God. Conversely, being a theologian of glory *is* being lost. The theology of glory "is the perennial theology of the fallen race."[72] This theology is related to our sinfulness not only as a symptom of our fallenness; holding such a theology is the definition of sinfulness. The cross causes us to recognize that we have crucified Christ, that our sins have wrought his cross. Yet in the cross, where one stands condemned and is brought to give up on oneself, then and there the sinner is claimed by God and raised to new life. The cross does not stand apart from resurrection. Forde states, "The word 'cross' here and in the entire treatise that follows is, of course, shorthand for the entire narrative of the crucified and risen Jesus. As such it includes the Old Testament preparation, . . . the crucifixion *and* resurrection."[73]

Forde divides the *Heidelberg Disputation* into four parts. The treatise begins with reflection on the law of God and the judgment it brings and ends with the love of God. The *Disputation* itself literally moves us from life under the law to new life in the love of God. Yet it does not do so lightly or superficially, but by moving us through a process of despair and subsequent hope, of death and then life. The *Disputation* operates on us in the following phases:

1. The Problem of Good Works (Theses 1–12)

2. The Problem of Will (Theses 13–18)

70. Ibid., ix.
71. Ibid., 3.
72. Ibid., xiii.
73. Ibid., 1 n. 1.

3. The Great Divide: The Way of Glory versus the Way of the Cross (Theses 19–24)

4. God's Work in Us: The Righteousness of Faith (Theses 25–28)

The section on the problem of good works addresses "the basic question of the Disputation. . . . What advances sinners on the way to righteousness before God?"[74] Through these theses, the theologian of glory's attachment to good works as the means to righteousness is mercilessly attacked. The law of God brings demands against persons and judges them guilty of relying upon their own selves rather than upon God. Not a person's evil, but their claims to any intrinsic or self-achieved righteousness are attacked. Not our evil works, but those which appear to be our brightest and best, are the grounds of our condemnation. God does God's alien work upon us, so that later God's proper work can be accomplished. God's wrath comes out against the theologian of glory full force. This wrath of God is real and prevents us from sentimentalizing our understanding of God. Even as self-reliant sinners see their own works as beautiful, these attacks of God, God's alien working on us, seem ugly and evil. We would deny them or at least claim that God is not "guilty" of this attack. Yet, we have it all wrong.

What we consider beautiful, our good works, are in actuality deadly. This sin is deadly because it "separates and seals us off from God. That occurs when the apparent goodness of our works seduces us into putting our trust in them. . . . We are in reality then, not just in theory, sealed off from grace."[75] Only fear of God in the recognition of the deadliness of our living offers us hope. "When then are the works of the righteous not mortal sins? When they fear that they are!"[76] This first movement offers twelve punches that seek to destroy all creaturely confidence in good works.

In the next set of theses which Forde characterized as dealing with the bondage of the will, Forde shows how "Luther turns to the subjective side of the question."[77] Even after the old Adam or Eve, that is, the theologian of glory, recognizes the uselessness of good works, he or she

74. Ibid., 23.
75. Ibid., 37.
76. Ibid., 39.
77. Ibid., 49.

will continue to hold to some bastion of human participation in the advancement toward righteousness. ". . . [W]e always come back to the question of the 'little bit' [we might contribute], one of the telltale signs of the theology of glory."[78] Only when this bastion is also destroyed, can we let God be God. We refuse to allow God to act unilaterally. We chip away at the totality of grace brought to us solely from God's side. There must be some way that we advance our way toward God. Some merit, however small, must sway God in our direction. In the face of the God who saves by grace *alone,* the "fallen will cannot accept such a God. That is its bondage."[79] In the recognition of our bondage, we begin to hit bottom. We know that without intervention we are indeed lost.

Finally in thesis 16 another possibility presents itself. For the first time, Christ is mentioned. "When the theologian of glory has finally bottomed out, Christ enters the scene as the bringer of salvation, hope, and resurrection."[80] Hope is available, when we "utterly despair of our own ability" and allow God to do the deed to us and for us.

This brings us to the part of the *Disputation* that has commanded the most attention throughout history. Forde titled these theses the great divide. Forde points out, accurately I believe, that the leap directly into these theses has resulted in misunderstanding.[81] When one moves into these theses without first being addressed by the critique of works and will, the result is the linguistic slip up that he warned of earlier. Suddenly, for example, thesis 21 wherein we are told that a theologian of the cross "calls a thing what it really is" becomes a call to critical realism, rather than a calling of sin and sinners what they really are in the presence of God. This leap to thesis 19 and following robs the *Heidelberg Disputation* of its attack on the theologian of glory. The first theses are necessary to bring the theologian "to a real existential crisis."[82] Forde emphasizes that the *Disputation* speaks here not of "theologies" but of "theologians." The question in play is the existential state of the theologian in the presence of God.

78. Ibid., 50.

79. Ibid., 53.

80. Ibid., 60.

81. Ibid., 69.

82. Ibid., 70.

These central theses pick up the mention of Christ from the earlier thesis and ask what Christ and him crucified reveal to us about God. Theologians of glory "see" the "invisible things" of God. Forde observes that "seeing" the "invisible" is an oxymoron.[83] They claim to see "through" creation or divine action to a "sea of abstract universals."[84] But they will find only the threatening presence of God there and no consolations for their troubled consciences. This threat, as we have seen, is real and should be terrifying. The only way this voice of accusation can be silenced is by the cross. Looking through the cross into the beyond will not help; one must look at the cross itself where Christ hangs dying for us. True, salvific knowledge of God is there on the cross. Through this theo-logy, this word of cross, God saves us from the terror. "The cross therefore is actually intended to destroy the sight of the theologian of glory. In the cross God actively hides himself. God simply refuses to be known in any other way."[85] By suffering and the cross, the sinner comes to know God. And "the suffering Luther has in mind first and foremost is the result of God's operation on the sinner."[86] In what Luther called *Anfechtungen,* the "terrors of temptation" and "the pangs of conscience" God is finally known.[87] When this God is clung to in faith, we finally "*suffer* this unilateral action of God."[88] All theorizing, then, can finally stop. "Knowledge of God comes when God happens to us, when God does himself to us. We are crucified with Christ (Gal 2:19)."[89] We are, in this process, totally passive, while God alone is acting upon us. In Christ, God sets aside the law, silencing it. It can no longer bully us about. The law's jurisdiction ends where Christ's begins.

The final section of the *Disputation* turns to the righteousness of faith. We have now had our attachment to the law, good works and the claims of the will stripped away. We have been turned to Christ crucified. This brings us to the end of the *Disputation* and to the creative love of God. In the cross we come to know that God loves the unlovely

83. Ibid., 72.
84. Ibid., 73.
85. Ibid., 79.
86. Ibid., 86.
87. Ibid.
88. Ibid., 87.
89. Ibid., 90.

and thus *makes* them lovely. We have been crucified now to be raised. When the old Adam or Eve dies and is raised, we spontaneously turn to the neighbor in works of love. Knowing that God has done everything necessary, we move out in freedom. We see the "bad, poor, needy, and lowly" whom the theologian of glory cannot see. "They don't even show up on the scale of values and are not regarded."[90] But theologians of the cross know that they are sinners and know their own poverty, yet they trust that the love of God creates precisely out of nothing. Finally, "The presupposition of the entire Disputation is laid bare. It is the hope of the resurrection. God brings life out of death."[91]

Forde treats the *Heidelberg Disputation* as much more than a theological treatise; he understands it as an actual proclamation of the gospel and therefore an actual doing of the gospel. This is its excellence. It does not simply describe the cross or God, it—to use the necessarily awkward phrasing—crosses or does God to the reader. Theology at its best must serve this purpose; "theology is for proclamation."[92] Proclamation is the final move, the logical, ultimate step of comprehending the things of God. When the shape of God's love is truly understood, we freely and spontaneously have to share the good news. To proclaim God's love is to end—as both *telos* and *finis*—the argument. Forde says:

> Theologians of the cross therefore come to understand that the only move left is to the proclamation that issues from the story. The final task is to *do* the story to the hearers in such a way that they are incorporated into the story itself, killed and made alive by the hearing of it.[93]

Proclamation, as for Ebeling, is what ultimately matters in the theology of the cross.

> Through the *preaching* of the cross in the living present, not through theological explanations, we are defended from the terror of the divine majesty. Precisely against the threat of supposed divine timelessness and immutability we are claimed in the concrete word of the cross in the living present; through baptism and Supper we are washed and fed. We feel and taste

90. Ibid., 114.

91. Ibid.

92. Forde, *Theology is for Proclamation.*

93. Forde, *On Being a Theologian of the Cross*, 13–14.

the truth in the here and now. To believe means precisely to be claimed by the cross and its word, to cling to that and find one's assurance there. The "solution" to the problem of God, that is, is not in the classroom but in church.[94]

The concerns raised at the end of the section on Ebeling are equally fitting in response to Forde. If anything, Forde's approach is even less historical. Forde's reading of Luther has God standing over and against all of humanity in an undifferentiated way. All alike are prone to the same temptations of glory and power. This is Forde's appraisal of how the theology of the cross functioned in Luther's day, but Forde carries it forward to today. Luther speaks across centuries of history directly to us. Time and time again, generic humanity is gathered up into the homogeneous "we."

Once again the neighbors in need do not enter until the last pages of the book. Even then, they are quickly dismissed. Having noted that "the theologians of glory try to see through the needy, the poor, the lowly, and the 'nonexistent,'"[95] Forde makes a glorious move himself, subsuming the needy, the poor, the lowly and the nonexistent into the category of "sinner." Through the quick move to generic categories, Forde renders the poor once again invisible. They get lost in a crowd of undifferentiated humanity. The theologian of the cross becomes another theologian of glory.

Sacramental Theology of the Cross

Peura

Out of the dialogue with the Eastern Orthodox Church, Scandinavian Luther scholars have come to a new understanding of Luther's theology including his theology of the cross. They have focused on his early years so as to emphasize certain aspects of his theology that most clearly lie in continuity with medieval theology. The Finnish scholar Simo Peura's book *Mehr als ein Mensch?*[96] is a contemporary example of this approach. His understanding of the theology of the cross will be dramatically shaped by his work on Luther's very earlier material.

---

94. Ibid., 75.

95. Ibid., 114.

96. All translations mine for Peura, *Mehr als ein Mensch?*

To begin to understand Luther, Peura looks at his Psalm commentaries from 1513 to 1516. From this period, Peura articulates Luther's
understanding of the deification of the Christian. Here Luther's dependence on late scholastic theology comes to the fore. Next, Peura looks at
how this theme is upheld in relation to the themes of justification and
God's love as they are articulate by Luther in his 1515 and 1516 commentaries on Romans. Finally, Peura comes to our theme, considering
the theology of the cross in light of deification. His basis for that study
are texts from 1517 and 1519. While the third part of his study will be
of most interest to us, we will need to retrace the steps his steps through
deification since that dramatically shapes his own understanding of the
theology of the cross. Without this background, it is difficult to comprehend how he could end up at such a different place than Forde and
Ebeling.

In the early studies on the Psalms, Luther presents his understanding of deification. In the act of becoming flesh, God in Christ deifies the
Christian. God bestows on the believing Christian his divinity understood as his "truth, wisdom and goodness."[97] Alternatively, God's divinity can also be understood as "his name" which is Christ himself.

> The above-mentioned determination of spiritual goods and of
> the name of God contains also an aspect that aims at the deifica-
> tion of the person (*deificatio hominis*). God is the whole bless-
> edness of *his* saints; the name of God gives the Christian the
> goodness of God, that is, God himself. The spiritual goods are
> gifts of God (*donum Dei*) *in* the Christian. The attributes do not
> remain, therefore, simply in God; rather they actually are given
> to the Christian.[98]

This means that there is a three-fold coming of Christ the word to the
believer. First and foremost, in the incarnation God becomes human.
Next, the word comes as grace (*Gnade*) heard and clung to. Finally, the
word takes form within the person as the gift (*Gabe*) of Godself. "In each
of these, the arrival of Christ—though differently in each case—has the
result of the deification of the person," argues Peura.[99] The thrust of his
claim is that God in Christ offers two benefits: grace (the merciful dec-

97. Ibid., 47.
98. Ibid., 48.
99. Ibid., 51.

laration that makes the sinner just) and gift (the *ontological* presence of God in the believer.) The first benefit has been the exclusive emphasis of Ebeling and Forde; the second is the reframing of God's benefits offered by the Finnish Luther interpreters. When God gives the sinner God's own name, God really and truly offers God's essence to them.

Luther also uses other terminology traditionally related to deification to make similar points. He speaks of participation in God, union with God, and the transformation of the person. "Through them all, however, the same point is legitimately made, that is, the actual-ontological character of the salvation realized by God in the person."[100]

This leads to Peura's work on Luther's understanding of justification. Simply stated, Luther comes to understand justification as the basis for the internal structure of deification. The emphasis on justification protects the sovereignty of God. The gift always remains a divine gift, but this gift is really and truly received by the Christian due to the grace of God. The gift is not due to extortion on the part of the believer; the motive for the giving is located in the same God who gives through the word. The reason for the giving is not, therefore, to be found within the Christian. In fact any preparation within the believer that makes possible the act of reception is also the act of God through the word. Peura writes:

> Luther understands God working in the word in a way analogous to God's relating at the cross. God executes his work on the person in the same way that God has done so already to Christ. The persons must, if desiring to believe and assume the word, first become weak and foolish in order to be able become strong and wise in the power and wisdom of God. Glorification and exaltation presuppose kenosis and abasement.[101]

Through the word, God destroys the self that is a self-justifying self; the sinner is reduced to nothing.[102] Through this reduction God creates a vacuum wherein God makes the person capable of bearing divinity.[103] God bestows God's name through a happy exchange as the sinner clings to God in faith and, solely by that faith, God justifies the

---

100. Ibid., 295.
101. Ibid., 113.
102. Ibid., 194.
103. Ibid,, 120.

sinner.[104] Justification results in the real transformation of the person as the name of God, which is God's essence or divinity, comes to reside, and this truly, in the Christian. This indwelling is not only founded in externality. The "real presence of God" indwells the believer as that person also dwells in the Godhead through participation (but not fusion) in the same. This transformation is integral and includes even the transformation of the human will together with other faculties such as the intellect.

> Transformation realizes itself in this life above all through the faith that transforms the faculties of the person and leads him to knowledge of the divine will. Transformation thus refers to how—already at justification's beginning—the whole person is renewed with his will again and again. The transformation of the will is important, because only thereby can the love of the new person increase.[105]

The transformation of the Christian leads to a new way of relating to God from the human side of the relationship:

> The *caritas dei* works in the Christian so that the person wills and loves what the intellect has allowed him to comprehend. The love of God for the person changes the person who then loves God willingly and seeks God again and again. For that reason Luther understands here by the love of God a constant affection (*affectus*) for God.[106]

So a new being that is ontologically transformed has been bestowed upon the believer, and this gift yields a new activity. The being of God within the Christian translates into a new doing wherein the deified Christian loves with the actual love of God; put another way, the God who is ontologically present in the believer becomes the subject of his or her actions.

Peura's interpretation of Luther differs dramatically from those we have already examined, yet he does claim as emphatically as they did that Luther's theology is a theology of the cross. Deification does not nullify the theology of the cross, but rather is the firm foundation upon which Luther built his theology of the cross. In what sense does

104. Ibid., 156.
105. Ibid., 157.
106. Ibid., 160.

Peura see the confession of Luther's theology of the cross within this framework?

First of all, the theology of the cross is a critique of certain aspects of scholastic theology since that theology of glory seeks to ground itself in a capacity that humans by nature possess. Peura writes:

> According to Luther, the *theologia gloriae* leads inevitably to the false striving of the person to deify himself. This way of thinking rests upon assumptions of natural human capacity and finally on the idea of *liberum arbitrium*. Thus Luther sees in the *theologia gloriae* an intensification of human sin, because, at base, it would like to realize its own egoistic, self-willed aspiration to divinity.
>
> By no means does it follows from this criticism of the *theologia gloriae* that Luther also rejects the true deification of the person as willed by God. On the contrary, over and against his criticism of the metaphysical basis for the theology of the love held to by the aristotelian scholasticism, he demonstrates that true deification (in the sense of an ontological transformation of the person) is the *conditio sine qua non* for true love.[107]

Thus the theology of the deification in Luther is also a theology of the cross because it sees God as the sole source of transformation.[108] Though this transformation is an actual, ontological transformation of the person, it is so not as a human act, but as an act of God alone. The error of the scholastics was to attribute to innate human capacity what can be done in humans by God alone.

This first characteristic, that is, that God alone justifies and deifies, has implied the second characteristic that qualifies Luther's theology as a theology of the cross. If God alone deifies, then the human being is not the subject or agent who brings about that deification. Thus, the word's act of reducing us to nothing destroys all attempts at *self-justification*. God again creates out of nothing, and, in this case, through the word, God is also the creator of nothingness. The human being has no grounds for boasting in the gift that dwells in him or her, because that gift, even when received and rooted, never loses its givenness.

Next, this focus on deification does not lead to a theology of glory, because the theologian of the cross knows that the deification truly

107. Ibid., 178.
108. Ibid., 270.

present is a hidden reality and remains so throughout earthly existence. Deification is not apparent to sight, though it has actually occurred. It is hidden under the opposite, that is, under the reality of the believer who is also a sinner. Only faith living under the sign of the cross is able to make the profession that God is certainly within the Christian bringing about deification.

Finally, the theology of the cross is manifest in that deification is a lifelong process of divine activity that is not ended until death and even beyond. People of faith recognize that sin remains within them even though they truly are united with God, and this recognition of their own sinfulness turns them outward toward God and the neighbor in need. This recognition of sin is so strong in Luther that he takes the descent into hell with the utmost seriousness, believing that one really does descend to hell, but that one is utterly and really transformed when in that very place God is present *with* and *in* one in hell; and this presence of God is a gracious presence wherein God is there in order to love transformatively.[109]

Luther held in short an "ontology of the cross" that recognized that *God* makes the Christian "*mehr als ein Mensch,*" thus the title of Peura's book. The divinely transformed person is more than human on the basis of God's indwelling. Peura is quick to add that Luther was not interested in specifying more than this about the meaning of the "more."[110]

The threat to Forde and Ebeling's approach that this interpretation poses is clear. Peura makes this explicit in his summary of his research. He writes:

> interpretations which leave the real, ontological character of Luther's thinking more or less out of consideration, cannot explain important intentions of the reformer satisfactorily. The deification of the person is not adequately understood as a phenomenon, when the being of God and the being of the person are grasped in exclusively relational terms (the relating of conscious "being", cognitive or otherwise) nor when they are grasped in a way wherein the one being is and remains definitively outside of the other. . . . Luther's thought form contains a certain ontology that can be identified neither with the modern personalistic, relational thinking nor with the middle

109. Ibid., 301.
110. Ibid.

age's substance metaphysics. This study confirms the interpretation according to which Luther's ontology is understood as
an expression of a "real, ontological" thought form (Mannermaa
1989, 189–192) or, as it has been described, as an "ontology under the cross" (Forsberg 1984, 179). From the point of view of
deification, this ontology implies a way of being that presents
itself as standing in strong tension with human understanding:
deification as being in God through participation in him is being in nothing of one's own.[111]

Peura's work is dramatically different from, and even contradictory
to, that of Forde and Ebeling. Although he helps us to see things that
had not been seen by the others, he does not help us in seeing Luther's
theology of the cross in its broader, historically-embedded context. The
challenge that Luther brings is formulated in light of conflicts in ideas
alone; the Reformation seems to be a clash of ideas or even, more specifically, ontologies. The public nature of the Reformation itself is lost
in the process.

Though the interpretation of Luther lacks the interest in social
context and reception that drives this study, it could provide some resources for the constructive challenge stated at the outset of ending the
divorce between history and spirituality. This contribution could come
by way of Peura's confession that there is a real, actual presence of God
in the person and thus in history. Though it is not the direction that
I will take, the confession that God's relationship to the world is not
simply external, but is an actual ontological presence, might provide
others constructive resources for addressing this same challenge in a
different manner.

On a personal note, what first drew my attention to Peura was the
way he offers an alternative to the near total dominance of Ebeling's
interpretation in Luther studies. The content of Peura's interpretation
does not lend dramatic assistance to my own program, nor do I at the
end of the day find it compelling. Yet the dynamic challenge that Peura
throws at contemporary ways of reading Luther opens a space of legitimacy for other alternative approaches. Peura's attention to neglected
or denied elements of Luther (indwelling, participation, deification)
and the resultant re-reading offer hope to others like myself who have
seen something different in Luther than generally has been observed.

111. Ibid.

Peura and others amenable to his position have prepared the field of Luther scholarship for power shifts in the realm of interpretation. This resembles part of the dynamic that Luther unleashed in his own day's field of discourse.

Prenter

Although Regin Prenter's writing ante-dates the work of Peura, and though he is not as immersed in Luther research as a vehicle of ecumenical association with the Eastern Church, he does share some of Peura's attentiveness to the sacramental presence of God in the lives of the faithful. In his brief article entitled "Luther's Theology of the Cross,"[112] Prenter articulates the need for connection between the historical cross of Jesus Christ and those crosses that we bear in our own historical lives. He writes, "This mysterious identity of the cross of Jesus Christ on Golgotha with our own is the *essential element* in Luther's theology."[113] In light of this assertion, Prenter asks about the ways that Luther's theology of the cross has been carried over—or, rather, not carried over—in contemporary theologies. He sees two ways that this "inseparable union" is denied in contemporary theology.

In Bultmann, Prenter sees a "theology of the cross without the word," meaning a theology of the cross that may speak often of the word, but that allows the present now of existential decision to swallow up the importance of Jesus, the incarnate and crucified word. The rootedness in Jesus' cross on Golgotha is forfeited and thus "[t]hrough this existentialist understanding of faith, the whole historical content or the historical basis for faith is made irrelevant."[114] Prenter offers a scathing criticism of this collapse into the present moment.

> The existentialist theological interpretation is the modern version of a theology of the cross without the word. The fact that existentialist theology and preaching often refer to the "word of God" and to "proclamation" does not alter the situation at all. In the existentialist interpretation, the "word of God" is no longer the apostolic gospel, which in the name of God bestows salvation to the believer through these historical acts, but is merely the presentation of a particular possibility of existence, an un-

112. Prenter, "Luther's Theology of the Cross," 222–33.

113. Ibid., 224 (emphasis mine).

114. Ibid., 226.

derstanding of existence which functions only as a challenge to the individual to choose this form of existence as his own.[115]

Luther's focus on the forgiveness made possible through the vicarious suffering of Jesus tragically is lost in this theological trend. Bultmann and others have forgotten the scandalousness of God's identification with human crosses through the cross of Jesus; the connection, when not altogether ignored, is made too lightly.

> We must never forget what an unheard of boldness it is, to iden-
> tify our own cross with that of Christ. When we consider the
> events of the passion, for example, it is almost blasphemy to
> mention our crosses in the same breath with that of Christ. It is
> certainly no foregone conclusion that such a thing should even
> be allowed, and it is only allowed because of the freedom which
> the child of God enjoys, given to us as a gift through our accep-
> tance in faith of that redemptive act of Jesus Christ in which he
> suffered vicariously the punishment for our sins.[116]

As a comment on the then current interest in the theology of the cross, Prenter makes an important observation about context. He ob-serves, "There has been a rediscovery of Luther's theology of the cross in our century precisely in those countries where the church must fight against a totalitarian state."[117] With this observation, he demands that the word of the cross not be threatened from another direction. For the theology of the cross without the word is not the only way that theolo-gians have sought to escape the historicity of faith. Modern orthodox theology has attempted to construct a theology of the cross upon the as-sumption of some kind of "two-realm pattern of viewing the world."[118] Contemporary Lutheranism demonstrates the danger

> that the theology of the cross may give way to the predomi-
> nance of a theology of the word without the cross. For where the
> church, as is the case in our modern secularized world, exists
> within the context of a strange, yes, perhaps even hostile world,
> she is always in danger of withdrawing into herself.[119]

115. Ibid., 227.
116. Ibid., 229.
117. Ibid.
118. Ibid., 230.
119. Ibid., 229.

If existentialism abandoned the historicity of the crucifixion of Jesus, orthodoxy stands in danger of turning from the historic reality of contemporary crosses suffered by humanity. In that paradigm, the only way that the cross is treated as contemporary is within the confines of sacred space, particularly in the preaching of the word within the context of worship. The intrinsic relationship between Christ's cross and our crosses is lost rendering the word impotent. In such a position:

> It appears as if the cross of Christ and our own cross belong only to a sacred world. We may preach constructively about it, but the historical reality of modern life seems to be a totally different realm from that in which the word about the cross fits, which consequently becomes something of a religious ideal, a theology of the word without the cross, not because it seeks to deny the cross, but because it no longer bears a living relationship to the cross in our daily existence.[120]

The cost of such a move is tremendous. The trinitarian God in the full sense has been denied. Christology so lords it over the entire godhead that not only false theologies of creation are abandoned, but also the true reality of God as Creator. When this occurs:

> There is no more room for God in history. Our world and our history have become godless, and our God has no world and no history. So now we have arrived at a point where the only history we still ascribe to God is the so-called history of salvation, the history of the second article, which implies a restriction upon the first article, as if God is no longer Lord of secular history, but only of the history of salvation.[121]

Prenter turns to Luther's work on the *Magnificat* to challenge orthodoxy's restriction of God's historical activity and lordship. In this commentary Luther holds history and creation together with the cross of Christ. When Luther addresses issues of poverty, he is speaking not of some spiritual poverty recognized in a sacred sphere, he speaks of actual, physical hunger and thirst as the medium of God's creative activity. He asks the reader:

> How do we come to identify the cross in the creation as the cross of Jesus Christ? Can we go along with this at all? And if

120. Ibid., 231.
121. Ibid., 231.

not, must we then not admit that Luther's theology of the cross
is not relevant for us?[122]

Again, Prenter returns to the theme of vicarious suffering. Christ suffers
on our behalf the cross that is laid upon sinners.

> As we in the course of our own lives experience the punish-
> ment for our fall into sin, through suffering, through tempta-
> tion, through death, it will become clear to us that, because he
> bore exactly the same on our behalf, because he, who possessed
> the power of divine love as no other human person lived and
> suffered for us—this all is no longer guilt and punishment for
> us, but the role of the children of God, which is permitted us
> through the gracious command of God in the gospel.[123]

He finally sums up the opportunity that Luther's theology of the
cross offers to contemporary theology:

> we must concern ourselves for both life and the word of God
> with like honesty and determination, so that we neither play life
> against the word, as in the case in a theology of the cross without
> the word; nor play the word against life as is the case in all sorts
> of thinking in terms of two realms such as occurs in the ortho-
> doxy entrenched in the church. For God is the trinitarian God.
> He is the God of life, the Creator; he is the God of the word, the
> Savior; he is the God of faith, the Holy Ghost, and this trinity as
> Father, in our common experience of life; as Son in the preached
> word; and as Holy Ghost, in our personal convictions, teaches
> us in the last analysis what it means: *Omnia bona in cruce et sub
> cruce abscondita sunt.* (All good things are hidden in and under
> the cross.) Therefore they cannot be understood anywhere else
> except under the cross; under the cross—that means, under the
> cross on which Jesus, our Redeemer, bore our punishment, and
> under the cross which my Creator has laid upon me in my suf-
> fering and in my death. For in both places we are talking about
> the same cross.[124]

In this short article, Prenter has brought us further along in our
task than the last three authors combined. His constructive critique of
the wedge driven between the cross of the incarnate word Jesus and the
other crosses in creation holds in appropriate tension our concern to

122. Ibid., 232.
123. Ibid., 233.
124. Ibid., 233.

not take the incarnate and crucified word out of our world. He offers us clarity in our critique of Forde and Ebeling who have taken Jesus' cross out of the realm of history. He reminds us that it is not an accident that people who suffer brutal abuses of power are turning to look again, not only with Luther but also with the original apostolic witnesses to Jesus, to the crucified Christ.

Critical Summary

We have explored three models of interpreting Luther's theology of the cross. In relationship to the concern that the theology of the cross be situated within the political and social history of its day, we appraise the three models differently. The third model offers some clues for bringing together theology and social reality. It does this by providing a way to talk about the theology of the cross in terms of the total context in which we live. Especially Prenter recognizes the God-given possibility and necessity of understanding Christ's cross always in conjunction with contemporary crosses. In the crosses of creation points of historical concreteness are provided in which Christ and context are related. One also could argue that Peura's emphasis on the real, ontological presence of God in the believer also provides a foothold for God's active presence in history.

The emphasis on the proclamation of the word in Ebeling and Forde, an element that the other two models also have noted to some extent, correctly identifies the nature of the Reformation as an oral event. Yet, the lack of interest in pursuing how that oral event functioned within the larger sixteenth-century context, including daily life lived outside of the church, robs what could have been a provocative historical observation of its force. The tendency, of collapsing historic distinctions through generic observations about humanity also speaks of the historical disinterest of this model. In Forde's writing, Luther speaks directly to "us" across five centuries. The shape of sin in the sixteenth century remains with us today without any interesting variation. Even within the sixteenth century itself, peasant and priest, pauper and king stand before God in basically the same way. It is amazing that such a strong critique of power like that which Luther offers can be examined to the total neglect of actual power relations between distinct members of society. Finally, even the neighbor and his or her cross only enters the picture at the very end of the process. Ebeling illustrates this when only in the final pages of the book does he raise as his last question the reality of those in need of compassion.[125] All of this indicates, as stated above, that Ebeling and Forde stand dangerously close to what Prenter characterized as a theology of the word without the cross. In their writings the poor are rendered invisible, and this is a sign of the theology of glory.

In my appraisal, the first model is best at helping us in our task of joining theology with history in the life and work of Luther. The recognition by Althaus and especially by Loewenich of the place of the institutional church and its abuses in the formation of Luther's thought addresses my concerns for contextual interpretation. Yet, even here the church is primarily thought of as a religious institution. The perception by the people of Luther's day that the church was a political, economic, and social agent of power is acknowledged, but this plays no significant role in the understanding of the shape of his theology. The next chapters will seek to redress this neglect.

One other comment needs to be made regarding all of these interpreters. They all reflect on Luther's development in such a way that historic distinctions inevitably dissolve in the rush to declare Luther an unwavering theologian of the cross. All of them claim that Luther is consistently a theologian of the cross throughout his career. A clearer exploration of the ways that Luther's theology of the cross took shape at different times in his life and ministry, as well as the ways that his practice diverted in significant ways from this fundamental commitment, might present us with a more accurate picture of the reformer and his theology. For example, one might ask how Luther diverted from the theology of the cross and its basic commitments in his response to the Peasants' Revolt. Similarly one might ask about how his theology of the cross functioned or malfunctioned in relation to the Jews of his day or in relation to divergent Protestant groups. Did Luther betray the theology of the cross in his own quest for power in relation to these and other groups? It is clear to me that the critique that Luther himself offered at specific times might be turned against him. There is a deep irony in the claim by Luther interpreters and followers that Luther was a consistent theologian of the cross throughout his whole life. The irony is that the claim that one is consistently a faithful theologian of the cross

125. Ebeling, *Luther*, 265.

sounds like the pious claim of a theologian of glory. For the theologian of the cross knows that she or he cannot maintain such unbroken faithfulness. Luther knew this profoundly and painfully in relation to himself. Yet he was able to rejoice that his own lapsing would direct attention to the one who alone is faithful, the God we know in Jesus Christ. In conformity to Luther's self-critique, we shall begin to critique him in his own historically embedded theological confession; we do this so that our own theological reflection might learn from his lapses as we speak to a new day. We also do this aware that, God willing, others shall so reexamine our lapses in the future.

Finally, the relative lack of interest in the questions posed here on the part of our six authors is not to say that I shall not use observations from each of these models as I pursue my own interpretation. Having revealed something of these diverse contributions, I am confident that the reader will be able to see the places where each has influenced my thought as well as the ways that I have broken company with them. We turn now to the task of mapping the context in which Luther lived and worked in order to understand how Luther's theology of the cross functioned therein.

## 2

Power Relationships in Reformation Germany

IN THIS CHAPTER THE MULTIPLE AND COMPLEX POWER RELATIONSHIPS of Luther's time will be explored in order to set the stage for reading Luther's theology of cross. Since Luther's theology of the cross explicitly attacks the abuse of power, acquaintance with the way power was structured in his world is essential to understanding his rhetorical tactics. Although this chapter will look at different domains of power like the economy, politics, and religion, they cannot be radically separated but are always intertwined. Take the example of indulgences. Their sales promised pardon in the presence of God, yet they originated because the church needed funding for its crusades. In Luther's day, the indulgence sales acquired the resources to pay off the Fuggers' banking company after it helped an archbishop and the emperor acquire their positions. The emperor, Charles V, then protected the Roman Catholic Church and persecuted Luther. All this to say that fine distinctions between economy, politics, and religion are impossible to make. Power from one domain often reinforced that from another.

In these complex lines of power, one thing remained clear. The church was consistently power-laden, whether the domain under discussion is political, economic, military, social, or religious. And conversely, the vast majority of the German population was locked out of the official mechanisms of power. In this context, religious critique was at least implicitly, and more often explicitly, social, political, and economic critique. Part of what drew the people to support Luther was his solidarity with the poor in the midst of these radical inequities.

Luther's Relationship with the Poor

The poor people of Luther's Germany welcomed his reformation at its inception. Precisely during this popular phase of the Reformation, Luther wrote his most concentrated and precise articulations of his theology of the cross. Is there some connection between these two points? Certainly several social groups found elements of Luther that served their own interests well. Might Luther have caught the attention of the marginalized peoples specifically through key elements of the theology of the cross? The theology of the cross itself calls for this mode of questioning in which the poor who are so often hidden from our sight become visible to us.

From the very beginning of the Reformation, Luther was either criticized or praised because of his popularity with the poor. Luther himself recognized the importance of his relationship with the poor for his theological proposal. Luther's self-understanding as a theologian of the cross was as a servant to the poor. He claimed:

> Thus my learning is not my own; it belongs to the unlearned and is the debt I owe to them. . . . Thus my wisdom belongs to the foolish, my power to the oppressed. Thus my wealth belongs to the poor, my righteousness to the sinners.[1]

Luther knew this commitment demanded listening carefully to the poor, common people. For example, when he worked at translating the Bible into German he emphasized the role of listening to the common people:

> We do not have to inquire of the literal Latin, how we are to speak German, as these asses do. Rather we must inquire about this of the mother in the home, the children on the street, the common man in the marketplace. We must be guided by their language, the way they speak, and do our translating accordingly. That way they will understand it and recognize that we are speaking German to them.[2]

Luther also described his preaching in a university town along similar lines:

---

1. LW 27.393; WA 2.606.4–10.
2. LW 35.189; WA 30(2).637.17–22.

> When I preach here I adapt myself to the circumstances of the
> common [*herunder*] people. I don't look at the doctors and mas-
> ters, of whom scarcely forty are present, but I look at the hun-
> dred or the thousand young people and children.... It is to them
> that I devote myself.[3]

Yet Luther's attention to the poor surpassed merely learning their
vocabulary and grammatical structure. They did not simply provide
him with a good audience. He believed that the poor of his day were
the ones most likely to grasp the call of the gospel in its unadulterated
clarity. He wrote, commenting on a verse from Jeremiah:

> among the great men one would find less understanding and
> justice than among the laity and common people [*gemeinem
> volck*]. Thus so is it now, when the poor peasants and children
> understand Christ better than the pope, the bishops, and doc-
> tors; everything is turned upside-down [*umbkeret*].[4]

Luther was not alone in the portrayal of his movement as the cause
of the people. Those who wrote pamphlets to promote the Reformation
also attempted to portray the movement's commitments as continuous
with those of the common people. Of course, the men writing the pamphlets were not simply describing reality, but were pitching a message
to the people. The fact that many pamphlets speak of popular support
for the Reformation movement in and of itself is not evidence that this
was so. Yet the pervasiveness of this theme in the broad pamphlet literature does indicate that Luther's preaching of good news to the poor
was a plausible and even persuasive theme, at least in the eyes of the
authors and artists. So, for example, a pamphlet from the early years
of the Reformation has peasants gathered in an inn proclaiming that
Luther is a prophet.

Another typical device used was to make the hero of a reformation
pamphlet's narrative an archetype of the common person. Numerous
times the pamphleteers made this pitch. One of the most prevalent images employed in this strategy was "Karsthans." Dressed in well-worn
breeches and peasant boots, shouldering his hoe or sickle, Karsthans

3. LW 54.235–36; WA TR 3, No. 3573. It is interesting that though this letter was
in Latin, he chooses to express some of the more weighty sections into the German he
speaks of in this citation.

4. WA 7.315.4–7, cited in Russell, *Lay Theology in the Reformation*, 60.

defended the gospel from the ignorance of the learned. He took on the studied priests with his simple understanding of the pure gospel (though that sickle did hang menacingly overhead) and left them in shame.[5]

Though the character changes, this motif is deployed in a pamphlet from the 1520s entitled *Dialogue between Peter and a Peasant*. Here the pure gospel exposes more than good news about eternal salvation, it exposes temporal oppression. In the dialogue, the peasant makes this accusation against Peter, "The pope's teaching is concerned about [extracting] the money and blood of the poor."[6] This kind of "common" sense is again hailed in a 1521 pamphlet entitled *Cunz and Fritz*. One of the common people points out the evil interests of the clergy. He summarizes the concerns of both the religious and the common people provocatively, stating, "He who has many benefices opposes Luther. . . but the poor folk esteem him highly."[7]

The same themes were applied visually in the drawings that accompanied the pamphlets. One drawing of this same period promotes Luther as Moses freeing the people from their bondage symbolized by a dark cave. While the poor move out to stand in the light of the crucified Christ, the religious hierarchy in this illustration defiantly place themselves on the same level as Christ. Their faces all are turned away from the cross. They stand vigilant over the cave of darkness that they had created. Within the cave, political authorities flee deeper into the darkness, refusing to follow Luther's gesture to the crucified Christ. Pamphlets containing the triad of peasant, Luther and Christ crucified are myriad during this period. We will explore one such pamphlet that bears Luther's stamp later in the book when we look at *The Passion of Christ and of the Anti-Christ*.

While it is possible to dismiss these portrayals as having more to do with the pamphleteers' propaganda interests than the actual interests of the common people, the common people themselves speak praise of Luther in the famous *Twelve Articles* of the Swabian peasants. The authors put forth Luther as a fair arbitrator of the dispute at hand; popular belief trusted Luther's commitment to the poor. While this hope was

---

5. Scribner, *German Reformation*, 19.

6. Hillerbrand, "German Reformation and the Peasants' War," 115.

7. Ibid.

not to be fulfilled when a real conflict erupted, the protesters who wrote
that tract indicate faith in Luther as a worthy and trusted spokesman of
their plight and interests during these early years.

The Reformation commitment to the poor grew out of the biblical understanding of God. Since this will be demonstrated later in the
book, one quotation suffices to confirm Luther's constant concern:

> God accepts only the forsaken, cures only the sick, gives sight
> only to the blind, restores life only to the dead, sanctifies only
> the sinners, gives wisdom only to the unwise.[8]

The conviction that God is the God of the poor and that the word of
God speaks most directly to the poor drove Luther to translate the Bible
into German and to write his own treatises in the vernacular so that
they would be accessible to the people. Luther almost relished the scorn
that some would heap upon him for writing in coarse German rather
than the refined Latin of official God-talk. In the early years of the
Reformation, he wrote to Christoph Scheurl that his own 1517 translation of the Psalms was not done with an ear for the sophisticated citizens
of Scheurl's city, Nuremberg, but for "raw Saxons" who could not digest
his theology were it written in Latin.[9] A few years later he continued to
comment on the disdain of the learned regarding the manner in which
he communicated, saying:

> And although I know full well and hear every day that many
> people think little of me and say that I only write little pam-
> phlets and sermons in German for the uneducated laity, I do
> not let that stop me.[10]

The actual expression of this scorn has been preserved for us in
the writings of Luther's opponents. Luther's fierce enemy Johannes
Cochlaeus complained about the effects that Luther's work was having
on proper relationships between the poor and the religious. He whined
that Luther's translations of the Bible were:

> so widely distributed by the printers and published in such large
> numbers that the tailor as well as the shoemaker, even wom-
> en and other simple people, could take in much of this new

---

8. LW 14.163; WA 18.497.37–40.

9. Brendler, *Martin Luther*, 85. See WA BR I 93.

10. LW 44.22; WA 6.203.5–7.

Lutheran gospel although they knew only what little [written] German they had learned from reading letters on gingerbread; the people read this Luther New Testament as the spring of all truth and with the greatest desire. Thus within months they [common folk] acquired so much skill and experience that they were bold enough to dispute about faith and gospel not only with the average lay Catholic but also with priest and monks, indeed with masters and doctors of Holy Scripture.[11]

This contempt heaped upon Luther in the early years of the Reformation only grew in light of the Peasants' Revolt of 1525. I find myself in an interesting situation now as I look back to Luther. Given my own sympathy for the right to revolt against oppressive situations, what once was uttered against Luther by his detractors now becomes evidence in his favor. The scorn cast upon the one who caused revolt has been replaced with my applause. Those who were against Luther might have overplayed his role as inspirer of revolt in order to serve their public attack on him. Nonetheless, with great regularity, the equation is made between Luther's Reformation and the peasants' uprising. Again, Cochlaeus's accusation is telling:

That the common man everywhere in Germany, except in Bavaria and Austria, is so mad and rebellious [aufrürig], is only the result of your own [Luther's] false and rebellious gospel. You have preached to the poor people so continuously and falsely of God's Word and Christian freedom until they became totally rebellious and mad.[12]

The emperor Charles V shares a similar opinion of the equation of Lutheranism and revolt. In his edict against Luther he wrote:

Indeed, he writes nothing which does not arouse and promote sedition, discord, war, murder, robbery and arson, and tend toward the complete downfall of the Christian faith. For he teaches a loose, self-willed life, severed from all laws and wholly brutish; and he is a loose, self-willed man, who condemns and rejects all laws.[13]

11. Cochlaeus, *Historia Martin Lutheri*, cited and discussed in Brendler, *Martin Luther*, 250.

12. Cited in Baeumer, "Was Luther's Reformation a Revolution?" 266.

13. Cited in Hillerbrand, *Reformation*, 98.

The powerful banker Jacob Fugger joins his voice to this complaint when he grumbled that "the new preachers proclaim that one should not observe man-made commandments."[14] That this equation penetrated the minds of many is illustrated in the off-handed defense of a priest in Urach. Johann Klass was accused of being a Lutheran while he was on trial for witchcraft. He defends himself, saying, "I have previously always opposed the peasant disturbance Lutheranism, and other sorcery and heresy, as befits a pious preacher and priest."[15]

The Peasants' Revolt was a historical turning point in terms of the peasants' support of Luther's cause. Having had their expectations lifted so highly, the descent caused by what as seen as the Reformation leader's betrayal was equally steep.[16] Luther's Reformation took a turn away from the common people as the common people turned from him in disappointment. This loss of popularity is understandable when one tallies up the human cost of the turn against the peasants. Roughly one hundred thousand peasants were slaughtered in the violent response of the authorities.[17] While Luther cannot bear all the shame for this bloody act that probably would have occurred without his encouragement, his complicity with the executers is worthy of blame. We will revisit this event in a later chapter.

In light of the hard feelings left on both sides, it is interesting that Luther does not defend himself by denying his role, and, indeed the word of God's role, in stimulating revolt. Over and over again, even after his betrayal of the peasants, Luther insists that proclamation will yield revolt. He openly states, "But let's be wise thanking God for his holy

14. Cited in Hillerbrand, "Reformation and Peasants' War," 124.

15. Scribner, *Popular Culture*, 267. This is his translation from archival research in Stuttgart. He references the trial record from April 26, 1529 in the following way: *Hauptstaatsarchiv Stuttgart*, A413 Bü 28, Nr. 6, p. 2.

16. My understanding that the Reformation movement as it evolved tended toward a kind of betrayal is by no means the consensus among contemporary scholars of the Reformation. In fact, the common appraisal, often by confessional Lutherans like myself, is precisely the reverse of my claim. For example, Leif Grane writes, "After the Peasants' War, the Reformation ceased having the character of a spontaneous, freely expanding movement, and was gradually transformed into a true evangelical church entity" (Graine, *Augsburg Confession*, 13). I realize my use of "betrayal" is not a neutral appraisal of the situation; however, I insist that "true evangelical church" is not less ideologically neutral.

17. Lindberg, *European Reformations*, 165.

word and give our mouth freshly to its blessed rebellion [*auffruhr*]."[18]
And in yet another,

> ... it should not affect us if the world, whose works we declare
> to be evil, judges that we are the most dangerous heretics and
> insurrectionists [*seditiosos homines*], overthrowers of religion
> and of the public peace, and possessed by the devil, who speaks
> through us and governs all our actions.[19]

Granted, Luther's understanding of revolt was different than that of
his accusers as well as that of our own minds. He could not embrace
a political movement that would overthrow tyrants by force. He saw
God entering history through the word of God in order to bring about
transformation. Yet his intentional use of this provocative vocabulary in
the face of the concrete accusations leveled at him is very intriguing.

At this point we will begin to sketch the economic, social, political, intellectual and ecclesiastical context of Luther's Germany. How was
power structured in and around that place? How did the poor suffered
in their conflict with the mighty?

Economic Power Relations

The Reformation took place in the murky moment that lay between
the once established and enforced model of feudalism and the capitalistic ordering of society that would eventually reign. The poor in
this moment experienced the worst of both these worlds, though the
shifting of systems also created some small, but open fractures into
which they stepped and inserted themselves as subjects in the historical
process. This happens not without precedent but with a greater level
of frequency and urgency precisely in the early Reformation. In 1521,
sixteen cities experienced unrest; in 1522, fifty-two cities; in 1523, forty-
four cities; in 1524, forty cities; and in 1525, the year of the Peasants'
Revolt, fifty-one cities experienced revolt.[20] The propensity for revolt
in this period indicates the intensity with which the common people
were grappling with the ordering of their world. They were seeking, if
only in limited manner, to redefine the shape of their world. In relation
to the Reformation, these revolts indicate the intense searching of this

18. WA 8.684.14–16.

19. LW 26.375; WA 40(1).573.11–15.

20. Brendler, *Martin Luther*, 256.

moment that resonated with the word Luther proclaimed. Luther formulated a response that was compelling not only for his own personal crisis, but also for his own people's social crisis. His personal crisis did not appear mysteriously in a vacuum; the political, economic, and religious climate helped to produce it.

Pure feudalism was itself in severe decline, though its backwash still flooded the land. Economic power was shifting from feudal lords to princely hands and the emerging financial bourgeoisie. With this, military power also ceased to be centered in the troops that feudal overlords had established in their interest to protect and conquer. Territorial princes now employed mercenaries to insure their increasing financial and territorial power. Yet, in many ways feudal domination of the peasantry still survived as the social and legal grounds for their subjection.[21] This continued domination is one of the sources of the revolts mentioned earlier. Eugene Rice notes:

> the sixteenth century was an age of permanent agrarian crisis. Where serfdom remained, it seemed a purely arbitrary bondage in a world where lack of personal freedom was no longer accompanied by any economic advantage. Free tenants resented all obligations and tried to escape the dues and services that landlords tried to enforce. Tension between landlord and peasant was endemic, and it occasionally erupted in open violence.[22]

This crisis of feudalism was brought about at least in part by a rapid decrease of the population as a result of the bubonic plague. One of the long-term material effects of the plague was to cause a crisis in agricultural supply and demand. Some of the lands that belonged to those whom the plague devoured became overgrown with forests; also larger landowners extended their holdings taking the adjacent land of victims. The amount of land dedicated to farming, as well as the number of independent farmers, dropped radically. This had a devastating outcome in a society in which grain was the main food source for the bulk of the population. Then later, the birth rate quickly overcame the mortality rate; within a couple of decades the population grew at an accelerated rate. In the years between 1500 and 1520 the German population increased from 9 million to 10 million. The population curve

21. Scott, "Economic Landscapes," 9.
22. Rice and Grafton, *Foundations of Early Modern Europe*, 75.

continued to soar upward on a trajectory that would eventually close the century at 16.2 million.[23] As a result, grain was much in demand and prices increased dramatically. The majority of the benefits of this change went to the large landholders. Meanwhile, the real wages of the laborers sharply declined bringing about a situation in which the gap between the necessities in demand and the resource available to a family to purchase them increased immensely. During the sixteenth century the cost of grain to the consumer increased by 255 percent while wages of the common people only increased by 157 percent.[24] So with the same amount of money, the peasant could only purchase a bit over half the food. Thus the widespread poverty became worse.

In addition small landowning families were further displaced as excess offspring who could no longer work the family holdings moved away. There simply were too many family members to work a limited amount of family land. So many went off to seek their fortunes elsewhere. Luther's father was displaced from his own family holdings and entered the mining industry. Yet he fared better than most. It was extremely common for members of the lower class to spend an extended period of time as domestic servants in order to accumulate enough money to marry and establish their own households.

The life of the poor peasant in this time abounds with contradictions. On the one hand, they served in an economic field that flourished, yet, on the other, their own existence did not improve but only got worse. In addition, their fate was in direct juxtaposition and contradiction to those who benefited from their labors. While a small segment of the peasantry began to prosper, the vast majority of their fellow farmers continued to live on only the most basic necessities. From the meager living they scratched out of the land, they had to pay dues to those above them.[25] Of course, the suffering peasantry was the vast majority of the population in Luther's time. Germany's population is estimated to be about 90 percent rural at the time.[26] The peasantry, like their poor counterparts in the urban environment, lived a very difficult existence;

23. Pfister, "Population of Late Medieval and Early Modern Germany," 39.
24. Rösener, "Agrarian Economy," 73.
25. Ibid., 74.
26. Scribner, *German Reformation*, 26.

they worked from the rising of the sun to its setting in order to do little more than survive.

The church of Luther's day had benefited for centuries under the feudal structuring of society. Brendler writes powerfully of the nature of the feudal church:

> the Church was also an exploiter. On its huge estates it held the peasants in feudal dependence and fleeced them not infrequently with the same indifference with which the secular feudal lords exploited their workers.[27]

The church's potential for feudal exploitation of the peasants within Germany was profound. The church possessed huge tracts of property across the entire German landscape. In some territories of Germany, the church claimed dominion of as much as one third of the land.[28] This, of course, affected not only the peasantry, but also those members of the lower nobility who lived with the powerful presence of the church.

Together with the continued effects of feudalism, early financial capitalism did its own work. An early form of industrial development dependent on and driven by capital investment appeared during this period. Production changes in the fields of textiles, shipbuilding, printing, and many other areas occurred.[29] During this time, Luther's beloved beer begins "its triumphant march into the front rank of German beverages."[30]

Mining, the industry of Luther's family of origin, provides a good example of what was happening within the framework of early capitalism to a variety of industries. Increasingly complex technology developed that made it possible to locate and mine ever deeper veins of ore. The model of family owned and operated mines gave way to ownership tied to venture capital. Whereas once family members harvested the surface and near surface materials, now increasing technology made deeper and more extensive mining possible. Yet the family owners could not pay up front for the required machinery, for the increased coal, or for the transportation from the mine to the smelting plants and markets. Thus, wealthier individuals or the growing banking firms such

27. Brendler, *Martin Luther*, 99.
28. Lindberg, *European Reformations*, 234.
29. Brendler, *Martin Luther*, 23.
30. Scott, "Economic Landscapes," 13.

as the Fuggers, would loan money at a significant annual interest rate. Those lenders who were not directly involved in the actual mining process enjoyed large-scale profits. They created a large-scale production system that converted labor into a commodity.

The Fuggers, a handful of European firms like theirs, and their investors became incredibly wealthy through this system of loan and collection. As a result of these systemic changes, the gap between the richest and the poorest people widened. Between 1511 and 1527, the Fuggers, more than doubled their holdings every two years. Their increase in monetary holdings also led to the possession of huge tracts of land.[31] This single enterprise literally controlled the economy of many areas of Germany. Royalty was, of course, among the chief investors. At one point in the 1530s, Duke George of Saxony owned seven hundred mining lots. By that decade, two-thirds of the state income came from dues paid to royalty on the silver mines.[32]

The Fuggers became entangled in political endeavors in other ways as they loaned money for bribes during the campaign for emperor by Charles V—five hundred forty-three thousand florins!—or the money required to purchase from the papacy expensive ecclesiastical positions—twenty-one thousand gulden in the case of Albrecht of Brandenburg's acquiring of the Archbishopric of Mainz. The revenues earned through indulgence sales financed Albrecht's ambitions. In fact, the Fuggers received as much money through the sales of Albrecht's Indulgences as did the building of St. Peter's in Rome![33] During this era, the Fuggers became the main banking house for the Roman curia's work in much of Germany, Scandinavia, Poland, and Hungary. This overlapping of political, ecclesiastical, and economic interests makes it impossible to draw clear distinctions between respective domains of power. The economic interests of these institutions were so intermeshed that Rice claims, "In Augsburg, in this first phase of its Reformation, the Lutheran attack on Catholicism was inseparable from the attack on monopoly and *Fuggerei*."[34]

---

31. Rice and Grafton, *Foundations of Early Modern Europe*, 52–53.

32. Wright, "Nature of Early Capitalism," 191.

33. Brendler, *Martin Luther*, 105.

34. Rice and Grafton, *Foundations of Early Modern Europe*, 184.

The Roman Catholic Church that had benefited from its advantages within feudalism, was also quite capable of perpetuating those privileges under the emerging capitalism. The papacy in this century had banking institutions like no one else and its financial resources were vast. Not only did it benefit directly from capitalistic ventures, but it reflected in its religious activities the framework of emerging financial capitalism, for example, in the practice of indulgences. Salvation and eternal life, as well as offices of the church, become commodities to be purchased and sold for the raising of revenues. Church profits inspired the people's prophets to raise their voice in protest. The church was decisively shaped by capitalism in both its internal and external relationships. The people saw this reality clearly. Historian Harold Grimm observes:

> By reducing many of its services to what amounted to money payments, the church became increasingly wealthy. As administrators of this wealth, many of the clergy, particularly the great prelates, gave a disproportionately large share of their attention to secular matters. It is no wonder that many townsmen looked upon the clergy as hoarders of wealth who drained their cities and lands of gold and silver. The poorer classes also often resented this wealth, as well as the tremendous power that the clergy exercised over them "from the cradle to the grave."[35]

Again, the effect on the poor caused by this whole economic system was devastating. The already existing contradictions become even sharper. Lindberg writes:

> The rise of a money economy created new social and religious issues and tensions. By the Reformation period cities were plagued by disunity, factiousness, and mutual suspicion due to increasing size and economic changes which raised social tensions to a new level. The expansion of commerce created both new wealth and new poverty.[36]

Thus the urban poor suffered with their rural relatives. The side by side disparities in wealth led to animosity and suspicion between various social groups. Though the cities and towns were places of new elite cultural contributions, they were also places of rebellion. As merchants

35. Grimm, *Reformation Era*, 15.
36. Lindberg, *European Reformations*, 39.

grew richer, and the chasm between the rich and poor grew more profound, the poor came to resent and even hate the wealthy.

One other change within the economic sphere had a dramatic effect, both internally on Europe and externally on worlds previously unknown to the Europeans. With the accumulation of capital, entrepreneurs began to gaze beyond the boundaries of their own lands. Capital became a driving force in the "discovery" and exploitation of resources hitherto unavailable for European consumers. By the time that the Reformation cause became public, the bridgeheads of European imperialism had been secured in the East.[37] This opened the way for exploitation of the Asian market and population. Simultaneously, the conquest of what has come to be called the Americas took place. Without the accumulation of capital and the change in market structures that allowed for profit driven exploration, Europe could not pursue the quest to conquer distant and unknown lands. The intra-European oppression of financial capitalism is exported as financial capitalism becomes international in its relentless pursuit of wealth.

Political Power Relations

As already indicated, economic and political power were bound together during this period. Those individuals and groups who wielded power in the political realm did so in the economic spheres as well; correspondingly, those denied economic resources were also denied political power.

Within Germany the territorial princes occupied the chief thrones of political power. Yet these princes represented no unified group since peculiar local and personal interests divided them. Unlike the other European nations, Germany was not driving itself toward a unified sovereign state. The territorial princes enjoyed great wealth as a result of the growth of capitalism. This allowed them to gather the resources necessary for the new military apparatus made possible by technological developments. Rice writes, "In no period before our own has the technology of violence been more fertile than in the century between 1450 and 1550."[38]

---

37. Rice and Grafton, *Foundations of Early Modern Europe*, 38.
38. Ibid., 11.

The development of new military strategies—built not around the cavalry of noble knights, but on armed common people—favored the more centralized and larger princely governments over and against the lesser nobles. The development of gunpowder as a ballistic tool deepened the possible threat of the common foot soldier with a firearm. With no concern for the celebrated, if not uniformly practiced, military virtue of chivalry, the commoner brought down the noble knight. He need not even look his adversary in the eyes! Thus the warfare was simultaneously "royalized"—given the prohibitive cost of weaponry and ammunition—and "proleterianized"—since once the weapon was in hand, anyone could pull the trigger.[39] The development of the cannon also occurs thanks to the metallurgic and mining developments mentioned earlier. This new technology of violence was one of the driving forces behind the more sophisticated mining of copper and iron. Thus the princely hands, joined again with the great banking firms like the Fuggers, benefited from the protection offered by these military developments as well as by the profits that their manufacturing yielded. This military power could not only allow the princes to face Roman threats without fear, but also could be used to squash internal revolts like those of 1525.

Germany as we know it did not exist as a single entity in the sixteenth century. The region that we now call Germany was sliced and diced into several hundred essentially autonomous political pieces. The lack of political unity was a curse when it came to standing against shared antagonists. This fragmentation allowed the institutional church to exercise its power and authority in a way that would not have been feasible in other areas such as France. Yet the very looseness of structure also made possible resistance to the church at a popular level since Rome could not simply woo and win over as its defender one ruler, but had to contend with a multi-headed beast that was Germany.[40]

Despite the political fragmentation, linguistic similarities united the people. In fact, the linguistic unity rather than twenty-first century boundaries defined Germany in this period. Even without a unified state, the population understood itself enough as one people to allow for a German sentiment to arise; they celebrated something like nationalism

39. Ibid., 15.
40. Brady, "Social History," 167.

without yet being nation. The people themselves spoke to each other about German heroes and enemies of the German people. They could talk coherently about German values or vices. And finally they could stand together, if at no other time, at least when they stood before a shared enemy. For many, the Roman Catholic Church represented such an enemy. Martin Brendler draws our attention to this resentment.

> The dependency on Rome was burdensome not only to the dynasties; it was a financial burden on the entire country. . . . What at first glance may appear as a matter for the ruling class is revealed on closer inspection to penetrate deeply into the entire population and to be interwoven into the entire social system.[41]

As Brendler makes clear, the papacy, the curia and the institutions of the church were not only religious entities, but also, in the strictest sense, political and economic institutions to be contended with in Europe and beyond. The pope was the monarch of one of the five chief Italian states. Clearly he was not as politically powerful as Innocent III had been a few centuries earlier; he did not stand unquestionably above all governors in Christendom. Yet he clearly stood with them. He had at his command a large military and naval force. The papacy had the funds necessary to function efficiently as a state. Harold Grimm writes:

> The pope, as the absolute ruler over the clergy and all the Church lands, ranked among the highest monarchs of Christendom, and his magnificent court in Rome became the envy of the most powerful kings. The cardinals, the high officials in the papal *Curia*, the archbishops, bishops, and abbots, and all the higher clergy throughout Europe lived on a relatively high social plane. Usually men of noble birth who had obtained their positions through political influence or by the expenditure of large sums of money, they lived on a par with kings and princes. This was particularly true in western Germany, where, for example, the archbishops of Mainz, Trier, and Cologne were also electors in the Holy Roman Empire and ruled their territories like kings.[42]

This royal collective that called itself the church was the most pervasive institutional force in Europe. It was an international institution like no other with the administrative forces to pursue its will. Popes and

41. Brendler, *Martin Luther*, 178.
42. Grimm, *Reformation Era*, 15.

other high officials formulated political policy, waged wars, and taxed all of Christendom. This power wielded by the papacy was not without grave cost. The papal see maintained its role as a political state at the cost of its role as a spiritual leader. Corruption rotted it to the core and no mystery needs to be invoked as to why a multitude of sources expressed such hostile feelings toward the church. Its fixation on political issues for the purpose of personal gain made the church not only in the world but clearly and decisively of the world. Corruption was unrestrained.

This corruption and politicization of the church on its international level was felt acutely in the case of the German territories. No ecclesiastical office of consequence was held without first paying a significant sum to the papacy, often with the help of the Fuggers. The offices themselves came to be held by those interested in increased familial power and dynastic expansion. Simony was widely practiced. As a result, the office holders were unqualified for the spiritual leadership of the flock. This fact itself was almost irrelevant since absenteeism was rampant.

As stated above, Germany was particularly susceptible to ecclesiastical exploitation since it was a highly fragmented region, completely lacking in the unity necessary to defend itself in the face of such a powerful lord. And so the money, the critics lamented, poured out of Germany, while foreign-born clerics and other office holders poured into Germany to exercise their authority over the Germans. Ozment notes, "No other land in the history of Christendom had allowed itself to come more under the papal thumb than late medieval Germany."[43]

Still other factors need to be brought into the exploration of sixteenth-century German political relations. The first of these is Emperor Charles V. He was elected at the dawn of the controversy between the Roman Church and Luther. His election left many financial and political debts with those who eventually became opposing parties. He was elected to an office that certainly held influence and power in an abstract sort of way, but that lacked concrete mechanisms to enforce his will upon the other sovereigns of the Holy Roman Empire. He was an emperor with no real empire but a fragile alliance of multiple and often competing political entities. Territorial idiosyncrasies in law, customs, and language divided what he would pretend to rule.

43. Ozment, *Protestants*, 11.

This lack of real structural unity and thus diminished power played an important role in the Reformation development. Though Charles may have wished to maintain religious conformity in his empire, he was effectively powerless to make this desire a reality. Scribner notes that when it came to enforcement, the emperor's hand was weak. For though the princes would not brashly defy the emperor, "simple non-compliance or non-cooperation of the princes" could frustrate the ambitions of the emperor and he could be "effectively reduced to impotence."[44]

Cities were also players on the political scene, further complicating the power relations in which Luther operated. Imperial cities in particular have drawn a great deal of scholarly interest in the past few decades due to their lively intellectual and cultural environment, their extensive records that the historian might peruse, and their incipient communal ideal that appeals to contemporary sensibilities. The imperial cities and their citizens enjoyed relative autonomy in relation to the princely powers. The relatively high intellectual, political and economic independence that the urban areas exercised made them places of vibrant activity. A deep but limited sense of the commune was celebrated among the citizens. Their politics was built on a contractual form of governmental power claiming that authority arose from within the citizens rather than being handed down from high. In actuality, though, those already endowed with power by their family name or accumulated wealth, that is, the patricians, ruled. Even citizenship in the cities was fully open only to adult, male heads of households; thus the understanding of who was truly a part of the commune was dramatically limited. The rhetoric extolling the common good masks the reality of a small group of rulers at the top of tiered structure. In order to enjoy any participation in the political process, the most important distinction was whether one was citizen or not. "Non-citizens were merely tolerated outsiders who participated in the social and economic life of the community only by permission of the magistrates."[45] Yet, the percentage of those in the towns and cities who would not count as citizens themselves was high indeed. When one considers women, the large percentage of domestic servants, Jewish people, and others excluded from the deliberation process and

44. Scribner, "Germany," 6.
45. Friedrichs, "German Social Structure," 239.

its authority, the pyramidal structure of this "communal" government is exposed. Urban tax records of this time show the unpropertied segment of the population, those thus referred to as "have-nots", could be as high as 75 percent.[46] What existed was an oligarchy that functioned democratically within itself in order to maintain its own very undemocratic privilege at the top of this pyramidal structure.

The analysis so far excludes references to the political power of the poor. This is no mere oversight, but indicates the actual exclusion of the poor from the political process. The vast majority of German people were able to express only an alternative operation of power within the existing systems through acts of revolt. As with economic power dynamics, so with political ones. The poor are marginalized if not outright excluded. Conversely, the institutional church of the day was well positioned in order to exercise control and authority in the political realm. It was located in a place of privilege that allowed it to be a chief rival or negotiator with other politically influential entities of its time.

Finally, this consistent imbalance was situated in a world changing in other ways. Political realities are suddenly and violently expanding. The leading powers of Europe engaged in a race to conquer and claim lands hitherto unknown to Europeans. Enrique Dussel notes:

> After 1492, *Europe* consolidates definitively in the sixteenth century and distinguishes itself from America, Africa, and Asia. The Islamic world from Vienna to Granada had hemmed in Latin-Germanic Europe until now. But now, for the first time, with the discovery of the fourth part of the world, America, Europe declares itself the center. The other three parts . . . commence their history as the periphery.[47]

Dussel speaks not only of geographic shifts, but of a political one. The European powers were consolidated in the very act of making the other parts of the world into a conquered periphery at the service of the imperialistic center. The church participated in this imperialism with the same forms of violence as other political and economic entities. When the conquistadors stood before the native peoples, they would read a *requerimiento* that painfully summarized the church's political ambitions.

46. Lindberg, *European Reformations*, 113.
47. Dussel, *Invention of the Americas*, 134.

> I require you to recognize the church as queen and superior of the world. . . . If you refuse or try to protract this process by malicious delay, I certify that with the aid of God I will wage mighty war upon you in every place and in every way. . . . I will seize your women and sons and sell them into slavery. I will rob you of all your goods and do to you every evil and injury in my power.[48]

As Luther centered his understanding upon the cross so did another who was born the same year as Luther, the conquistador Hernán Cortés. He too was interested in the symbol of the cross. The banner over Cortés as he went out to wage war on the indigenous people of the newly uncovered world bore the words: *We follow the cross and in this sign we shall conquer.*

Social Status and Power Relations

In addition to and often complementing the economic and political status (or lack of status) attributed to groups and individuals, social respect (or disrespect) affected one's ability to function effectively in one's community. This is particularly true of sixteenth-century Germany, which structured its society based on "estates" (*Stand*). Although people's estates were not necessarily fixed for the duration of their life, at any given moment everyone knew their status in relation to those around them. A modern social historian states the case succinctly, "The social ladder was complex, but people always knew which way was up."[49]

Society was divided into three broad categories: peasantry, citizens, and nobility. These were broken down into about one hundred different trades ("trade" being another aspect of estates). Yet such differentiations applied almost exclusively to urban dwellers. This means that 90 percent of the population was simply categorized under the general heading of "peasantry." The life of the peasant was described with the following little ditty: "By nature I am but a *Bauwr*, Work for me is hard and sour."[50] The appraisal of the peasant by other members of society was vicious. Lindberg notes:

48. Cited in Dussel, *Invention of the Americas*, 50.
49. Friedrichs, "German Social Structure," 247.
50. Ibid., 248.

the life of the peasant was hard, and not infrequently harden-
ing. The upper class frequently depicted the peasant as stupid,
coarse, loathsome, untrustworthy, and prone to violence. For
the nobles, of course, such self-serving descriptions rationalized
and legitimated oppression of the peasants.[51]

Within the peasants' own setting, status was complex. Some peasants held more prestige based upon their relative economic and social
standing in their smaller community. Status was thus related to whether
they owned land or worked on another's, whether they kept all their
own gains or had to pay dues to an overlord such as a nobleman or an
institution like a monastery. Yet even in the best case, the peasant's status lay at the bottom of the social ladder. A peasant was "but a *Bauwr*."

In the urban environment things were charted a bit more com-
plexly. As many as one hundred different trades could be deliniated.
Within the urban social ladder, the most important distinctions were
founded upon citizenship. The patricians headed up the elite of the urban environment. Slightly below the patricians in status were the merchants who had accumulated resources through their export-oriented
endeavors. Other professions also afforded one a great deal of prestige,
especially those that were marked by an advanced degree of education
such as that of lawyers, doctors, and university professors.[52] Often those
who were able to pursue these professions were sons of the patricians.
Thus their high prestige was the result of the conjunction of inheritance
and achievement.

Membership in various trade guilds also assigned a person status
in the community. Often public processions to celebrate holidays would
be lined up according to the status of one's guild. Within each guild,
status was also tiered. Craft masters were usually given entrance into
the citizenry, while this remained an aspiration for journeymen, and a
distant aspiration for the yet lower status of the apprentices.

Women were among those excluded from the full rights of citizenship. Their status during this period tended to be derivative of the
status of the males to whom they were attached; a woman's status was
based upon a combination of her father's status and her husband's, if

51. Lindberg, *European Reformations*, 33.
52. Friedrichs, "German Social Structure," 240.

she should have one. Thus, the influence a woman exercised upon the commune was generally indirect.

One group of non-citizens actually exercised high status within the cities even though they were not a part of the political commune. Priests, monks, and other clergy were exempt from citizenship. Yet this exclusion was not imposed from above, but was self-elected. This exclusion provided exemption not so much from the privileges of the citizenship, but from its responsibilities like payment of taxes, military defense of the city, and subordination to the civil legal system. This provided one source of the rampant anti-clericalism oft expressed during this period.

Finally, who held a place at the bottom of the urban social ladder? Together with the journeymen and apprentices, domestic servants made up a large percentage of the urban residents designated as "have-nots" (*Habenitse*) or the "underclass" (*Unterschicht*). Their lack of urban status flowed out of the lack of status prior to coming to the city; they were urbanites of peasant origin. In order to move toward relative economic independence, peasants worked in the city for a time. Their employer supplied room, board, clothing, and a stipend paid at the termination of their service.[53] Because of the late marrying age common at this time, the period of domestic service often lasted as long as twenty years.[54] These domestic servants made up roughly one quarter of the urban population during this time period.[55] Those who had experienced a phase of domestic service at some point in their lives would constitute an even larger percentage of residents since many had moved on to presumably better things. The status and prestige accorded a domestic was incredibly low. Not only did they live under the authority of another in their public life, but even in what might amount to their private life, they were under the constant vigilance, supervision, and sovereignty of the heads of household. Their lives were not their own during this extended period.

The nobility were at the top of this social ladder. The conjunction of ancestral status, financial resources, and political power endowed the nobility with a continual source of social status. The social structure

53. Wiesner, "Gender and the Worlds of Work," 218.

54. Ibid., 227.

55. Brady, "Social History," 268.

placed the Holy Roman Emperor, king, princes, and lower nobility near the top of the whole social pyramid. High ecclesiastical office holders occupied the pinnacle. The reason for this is clear. By birth these higher ecclesiastics already had the status of nobility. They were recruited exclusively from the ranks of the nobility. Their religious offices moved them a final rung up the ladder, yet their noble background positioned them to take that step. The combined force of these two characteristics placed them in the privileged position of what was known as "the first estate."

Again, the lower extremes of power and prestige were held by the poor and the higher realms included the official representatives of the church. However, the power conferred on the basis of status, even more than that based on political power, was often nebulous and open to alternative interpretation. For example, anticlericalism reconfigures status-based power relationships by offering a subversive interpretation of the status deserved by the clergy. Based on the perception of the oppression or hypocrisy enacted by the clergy, anticlericalism redefined and demoted the clergy status in the eyes of the public. The poor took on anticlerical attitudes that lowered in their minds the status of clergy who benefited from systems of oppression. However, this bias could also be used toward other ends by groups with motives different than popular interests. The patricians and others located near the top of the ladder deflected popular anger aimed at their many advantages by redirecting it at clerical privilege.[56] Thus, while anticlericalism was well-warranted, its liberative effects for the poor should not be overestimated.

Ideological Power Relations

The Reformation encountered an opportunity to surface through fault lines of economic, political, and social power in the sixteenth century. Yet, the power to formulate and disseminate a perspective on the world also was of fundamental importance for this movement. Ideological power relations were related to the political and economic ones, but they also had distinctive characteristics of their own. Several signs of the avid pursuit toward new forms of understanding surfaced in this period. The hegemonic influence of the grand scholastic vision had accompanied the church in its rise to power and ideologically had but-

56. Scribner, *German Reformation*, 39.

tressed that power. In the early sixteenth century its days of glory were numbered. Lohse writes, "By 1500 the era of great scholastic systems had come to an end. Thomas Aquinas and John Duns Scotus no longer dominated the field, even though their systems were still frequently held and taught."[57] This breakdown opened a brief window of opportunity for intellectual innovation in the church and even society to assert itself. In this lively environment, German universities grew. This in turn created a growth of the intelligentsia. Humanist movements sprang up primarily in urban areas offering them a new way of envisioning the world. The printing press entered into its own and book production and sales skyrocketed. A veritable flood of pamphlets challenged old ways of thinking and presented alternatives. Preaching flourished as a means of mass communication. Free travel of ideas through commercial routes disseminated ideas rapidly in print and oral form. Popular means of discerning and transforming reality also took the stage during this time. Within this volatile intellectual arena Luther's theology of the cross took shape.

German universities were among the spheres of society enjoying lively intellectual stimulation. In the beginning century prior to the Reformation only three young academic foundations had existed in Germany. By the time Luther was a young adult fourteen universities existed in his land. While the general Germany population suffered numerical declines during this period, student population grew by 500 percent.[58] This increase of university education created an exuberant intellectual environment that could not help but influence the larger context. Yet this growth was not without its problems. The growth in training was not met with an equivalent growth in suitable employment for those so trained. Thus a disgruntled, underemployed group of educators came into being, academically capable, yet unfettered by institutional allegiances. Scribner argues:

> one of the important preconditions for the German Reformation
> was a large pool of intellectual talent, discontented with the op-
> portunities available, and especially with a system riddled with
> pluralism, favoritism, simony and foreign (Roman) control.
> The robustness of German intellectual life . . . , therefore, was

57. Lohse, *Martin Luther*, 13.
58. Scribner, "Germany," 11.

matched by an equally high degree of discontent, even alien-
ation, among its intelligentsia.[59]

Among those helping to produce its share of the intelligentsia was
Luther's Wittenberg. As Elector Frederick's dream of a first-class university came into being, this small university experienced an explosive
influx of students. Luther's growing popularity drew them. In 1508, after
only six years of existence, enrollment at Wittenberg numbered three
hundred students. By 1522, two thousand students had flocked to learn
in this center of controversy.[60] This huge influx of young students made
dramatic changes to the city of Wittenberg. Not only was the student
body youthful, but the same could be said of the faculty. Early in the
last century, Reformation historian Herbert Schöffer claimed that the
Wittenberg faculty was "probably the youngest body of teachers in the
whole history of German universities."[61]

Though the Wittenberg professors might be held responsible for
the surplus in the intelligentsia, they also found a way to put them to
meaningful work. Many of those educated in the halls of Wittenberg
became parish pastors and found meaning in effecting reform and
stimulating thought at the grassroots, parish level.

Within the whole field of education, one group or movement has
drawn the attention of Reformation scholars and merits mention. The
humanists provided fuel that would enable the Reformation fires to burn.
They emphasized the need to return to the sources with their battle cry
of *ad fontes*. They developed important philological techniques as well
as critical editions of the scriptures and church fathers in their original
languages. And they developed the study of languages in order to read
those sources properly. By returning to the classics, they reinforced the
growing awareness that history is not static. They could see in the historical record that life had changed from what it once was. The world
was no longer imagined as the static entity; the world was in process, in
flux, capable of radical transformation.[62] By recognizing the historical
embeddedness of thought, the humanists were able to critique the way

---

59. Ibid., 11.

60. Spitz, "Luther's Social Concern for Students," 115.

61. Schöffler, *Die Reformation*, 82f. Cited and discussed in Moeller, *Imperial Cities
and the Reformation*, 33.

62. Grimm, *Reformation Era*, 51.

thinkers of their own day related to their own context. They, like Luther after and with them, aimed that critique at scholasticism. On the basis of the biblical sources they could call for an abandonment of that unnecessarily complex system of thought and a return to "true theology." The first generation of humanists paved the way for many of Luther's insights; and their students were among the most ardent students, and then teachers, of the Reformation.[63]

Yet the creation of ideas was not enough to transform the map of power. The words of the Chilean dictator Augusto Pinochet might have been spoken by those whom this new intelligentsia attacked, "We have nothing against ideas. We're against people spreading them." The printing press was the key medium for the spreading of ideas in written form. Scholars who examine this historical period continually call attention to the fortuitousness of the printing press for the Reformation cause. Richard Cole states, "The development of Luther's theology coincided exactly with the period in which European culture moved from the age of manuscripts to the era of printed books."[64] The printing of texts in the vernacular allowed for rapid dissemination of ideas over geographically distant places. The early Reformation represents this rapid flourishing of print materials. Robert Scribner notes, "At the beginning of the sixteenth century there were only about forty editions of works in German produced each year, yet in 1519 alone there were 111 new titles on the market. In 1523 there were 498 titles . . ."[65] The Reformation cause stood in the center of this intellectual whirlwind. Of the 498 titles published in 1523, Luther wrote an amazing third of them; of the nearly 500 titles, 418 were either by Luther, by his supporters, or by his opponents responding to him. Luther set the intellectual agenda for his age![66]

The writing of books opened up the possibility not only for rapid dissemination of ideas, but for intense conversation or argument between various writers. Luther, more than any other historic figure up to that time, had the opportunity to present his ideas to a large audience, receive their nearly immediate responses, then restate, reform or

63. Moeller, *Imperial Cities and the Reformation*, 33.
64. Cole, "Dynamics of Printing in the Sixteenth Century," 95.
65. Scribner, *For the Sake of the Simple Folk*, 2.
66. Ibid.

clarify his own ideas, only to repeat the process again. No other historic figure, especially one presenting an alternative to the status quo, could have participated in such widespread intellectual interaction prior to this moment. No wonder that those who had overseen ideological argumentation and dissemination in the past lacked enthusiasm for the printing press. Pope Alexander VI, the reigning pope at the turn of the century, already had foreseen the dangers inherent in the press:

> The art of printing, it is very useful insofar as it furthers the circulation of useful and tested books, but it can be very harmful if it is permitted to widen the influence of pernicious works. It will therefore be necessary to maintain full control over the printers so that they may be prevented from bringing into print writings which are antagonistic to the Catholic faith or which are likely to cause trouble to believers."[67]

With the rise of the printing press, concerted attempts at censorship come into history for the first time. This censorship was not only utilized by the church, but later by the anxious nobility in the wake of the Peasants' Revolt. Yet in the early years of the Reformation, the press was seen as serving the people's interests. Over and against the foreign domination of the church, the press supported German interests. This message was reinforced by the medium since the printing press was recognized proudly as a German invention.

At this point some caution is required. The explosion of print materials and formal education should not cause us to forget that 99 percent of the population did not go to the university and that only 4 or 5 percent were capable of reading Latin or German at any meaningful level. For women within the population the case is even worse. The few literate women would have been trained to read, but not necessarily write, since such self-expression was not considered virtuous, but rather dangerous. If they read, they could absorb the "useful and tested books" by male authors. But writing allowed for self-expression and subversive definitions of the world and womanhood. For a minority of women to take in the wisdom of men was virtuous, but for even a few to express the perceptions of their own minds was hazardous.[68] This is not to say that some women did not find a way outside of this social expectation.

---

67. Rice and Grafton, *Foundations of Early Modern Europe*, 10.

68. Wiesner, *"Gender and the Worlds of Work,"* 212.

Mechthild von Hockeborn was frequently quoted in devotional collections as was Gertrude the Great.

The impact of the printed word on women and the vast majority of the German population would not have been through direct, personal reading and reflection, but through the public reading of texts aloud, sermons based upon printed commentaries, or conversations that synthesized the material previously read by someone. Rather than a direct influence, the printed word probably impacted the broad community through a series of effects, beginning with the formation of opinion leaders.[69] Within the Reformation movement, for example, the word went forth in this manner. Luther wrote a treatise; the text was published and possibly edited by the printer; the text was read and interpreted by the parish pastor; it was preached *en toto* or in synthesized form as the preacher localized its message in light of his reading of the parish; the hearers of the word took it in and understood it in their own way; they went to the market and commented to a friend about what they were thinking; that friend kept the process going in a local tavern when he returned to the village. And so the chain continued on.

The process was more complex than the handing on and reading of documents. The dissemination of ideas took place through a complex network of oral, written, and printed communication.[70] This whole process was more complicated than a uniform, printed text would suggest. The role of the common people as interpreters and communicators unseats the exclusive sovereignty of the printed medium. Scribner is helpful here:

> Historians always stress the uniformity and authority of the printed word in creating coherent movement around a well-defined body of religious doctrines. However, if we examine the way the new ideas spread orally, we see that it was far less defined, far less coherent. Personal discussion of ideas enabled people to make their own choices of the ideas they heard, to impose their own understanding on them, rendering the content of the message more diffuse and complex.[71]

---

69. Scribner, *The German Reformation*, 20.

70. Ibid.

71. Ibid., 22.

A second very important form the print medium took was visual propaganda geared toward the popular community. This form, sometimes accompanied by printed texts, was directed at the majority of the population who read the illustrations. The content discussed earlier in this chapter corresponded to the medium itself. Pamphlet literature was characterized by

> drawing on several popular cultural codes: play and game, carnival, popular festival forms, insults, theriomorphism, grotesque realism and the demonic. These were all systems of signs readily recognizable to the common folk of the time. . . . The creators of the propaganda worked largely by taking these familiar signs and reassembling them as 'images in syntagma' which could then be read by the unlettered as easily as we recognize the visual allusions of television commercials today. However new the message they were presenting, the codes were age-old and customary. If Reformation popular propaganda was highly successful, it was because it relied so heavily on what was taken for granted in popular culture.[72]

The growth of pamphlet literature corresponds to the window of opportunity in other areas of ideological activity. Mark Edwards, based on the studies of the massive Tübingen pamphlet project, notes that in one of the early years of the Reformation, total pamphlet publications increased 530 percent. In the following six-year period production continued to increase another 800 percent. During 1524 alone, the year before the Peasant Revolt, pamphleteers published 16 percent of the pamphlets in the first three decades of that century. The dynamic early years of the Reformation from 1520 to 1526 produced 73.9 percent of the pamphlets produced in those three decades.[73] What is more, popular vernacular text accompanied the pamphlets' images. This represents a shift as German works increased during 1519 to 1521 from 25 percent of the pamphlets to 75 percent. 1522 trumped even this accomplishment as the presses of the empire put out a meager 10 percent of their pamphlets in Latin. [74] This represents more than a linguistic shift. German people rather than a minority of educated and often foreign-born elites were involved in intelligent discernment.

---

72. Scribner, *For the Sake of Simple Folk*, 94.

73. Edwards, *Printing, Propaganda, and Martin Luther*, 20–21.

74. Ibid., 21.

Those who could not read even the German words on these pamphlets were not irrational. Rather, they articulated, learned and "read" based on the different kind of symbol system that Scribner described above. A language, largely oral and/or visual, was interpreted and employed routinely by this vast German majority. The minority who were literate in written German and Latin could very well be uninformed when confronting the popular communication of the majority. The neglect of visual and oral communication as a source for theological reflection on the part of Reformation historians, finally being rectified in our day, is probably more due to our being visually illiterate than to the lack of clues and information contained within the visional images. The preferred medium of the twentieth-century scholar, the written text, has dominated our reading, rather than the preferred media of the sixteenth-century masses. Claims that popular communication presented simplistic or misconstrued understandings of Reformation ideals is actually grounded in our own inability to read the symbols rather than in the inadequacy of the communication.

Fortunately, historians have begun to unearth clues to the elements of the world that were misunderstood or ignored by previous scholars. Scribner has drawn together data about popular culture in this time that helps us to explore the formation and dissemination of ideas at the time of the Reformation even beyond the pamphlet literature. He has scoured legal records and uncovered accounts of popular communication in the form of "carnivalesque" activities. Following the groundbreaking work of Mikhail Bakhtin, Scribner argues that carnival is a "second life to the people."[75] This second life is manifested in acts that present a momentary yet real world in which the people can live and think in new ways. Scribner describes the characteristics of these popular acts of reinterpretation:

> Under this aspect the mockery, mimicry and parody of official life, culture and ceremonies seek to overturn the official world by exposing it to ridicule. The process is twofold: exposure of the official world, and robbing it of its dignity.[76]

75. Scribner, *Popular Culture and Popular Movements in Reformation Germany*, 88. See also Bakhtin, *Rebelais and His World*, 6.

76. Scribner, *Popular Culture and Popular Movements in Reformation Germany*, 39.

And again,

> Carnival presents an alternative world which upturns estab-
> lished authority and truth. These pretend to be ageless and im-
> mutable; carnival sets them firmly in the context of time and
> impermanence, showing them up as carnival dummies which
> can be destroyed in the marketplace.[77]

On the basis of a thorough search of civil records, Scribner located
twenty-four incidents in Germany between 1520–1543 where carnivalesque events came together with Reformation concerns. On the basis
of the Reformation's later turn from the cause of the common people,
it is noteworthy that nineteen of the twenty-four events occurred between 1520 and 1525. In these events, the people ridiculed the powerful
using satire and mockery to call into question those who would control
their space. They were brought to court for disturbing the peace and
challenging established authorities.

The social distance between the "learned" or literate and the vast
majority of the people stands out. Clearly, at least two different ratio-
nalities were active at the time of the Reformation. Yet focusing on the
large number of popular interpreters and the small number of elites
could obscure the underlining imbalance of power when it came to im-
plementation of the conclusions of each group's operational rationality.
The written letter, often Latin at that, was the basis of the law, diplomacy,
and public deliberation. Ability to read and write the official language
of the empire opened the door to the exercise of power. Literacy was a
cornerstone of social stratification.[78] In this dynamic, too, the church
hierarchy was once again positioned antithetically to the place of the
poor. As with economic, political, and social power relations, the church
hierarchy was ideologically power-laden. The church leadership sought
to keep interpretive power out of the hands of the rest of the people.

The growth of printing and universities, the lively expression of
ideas whether in books, pamphlets or carnivalesque acts, as well as with
the time of urban and rural unrest, all corresponded with the early period of the Reformation. The Reformation took shape during an incredibly dynamic time of intellectual grappling with the world, God and
human places within it on all levels. Within this context, Luther himself

77. Scribner, "Reformation, Carnival, and the World Turned Upside-down," 326.

78. Scribner, *For the Sake of Simple Folk*, 2.

struck a responsive chord, drawing together distinctive social movements, if only for a moment. Luther had stumbled into the pulpit of a
people craving transformation. Whether he intended it or not, Luther
became a public voice that gave ideological legitimacy to multiple and
diverse demands for a new order.[79]

The conquest of the so-called New World also played a role here
in the way that Europeans had come to understand themselves. The
conquest expanded the political and geographic world of Europeans,
but that is not all. Through the act of conquest, Europe established itself
at the center of the known world. This geographic and military transfer
of power is accompanied by a mental shift. Up to this time Europe had
sat at the feet of Greco-Roman antiquity and wisdom of the Near and
Far East. With the quest for conquest, Europe turns from that depen-
dency. Europe moves from having a cultural and intellectual debt to the
rest of the known world to being, in the words of Rice, "cultural creditors."[80] Latin American Enrique Dussel warns wisely of caution when
appraising the value of this shift. For if one dependence ended, the dependence of the indigenous people of the "New World"—a dependence
not chosen, but imposed by force—came into being. The metaphor of
"creditors" is ironically appropriate to Dussel's observations, especially
when the social cost extracted from the vulnerable by the likes of the
Fuggers is understood. Dussel's point is crucial; during the early years
of the Reformation, the European ego is constituted as conqueror by
conquering the "other." Charles V's empire and his beloved Spain not
only attacked Germany at the periphery of its empire, but turned to
create a new margin for exploitation.

Religious Power Relations

It may seem strange for a theological book to reserve the examination
of religious power until the end of a chapter exploring power relationships. This was done not because religion is unimportant, but rather
to show clearly how entangled religious institutions and their power
sources were with economic, social, political, and ideological dynamics.
In such a context, critique of the church was not only critique of a religious institution, but a simultaneous critique of an economic, political,

79. Brendler, *Martin Luther*, 115.

80. Rice and Grafton, *Foundations of Early Modern Europe*, 1.

social, and ideological posture of the church. Thus Paul Böckmann was correct when he claimed:

> Every theological point of dispute led deep into the basic structure of the entire political and social existence and in fact touched the life of the people in all its manifestations. . . .The disputes were not only about matters internal to the church, but concerned the total order of medieval life and thus a new image of the German person.[81]

The church, at least in its embodiment in Germany, had lost sight of its purpose of infusing the world with meaning and of creating a community of faithful Christians engaged in witness to Jesus Christ. The priesthood became turned in on itself and served the needs of the institution rather than the life of the people. The church became the possession of the hierarchy and they used its resources to serve their own needs. When the pope who ruled through the Reformation's beginnings had taken office, he is rumored to have summed up the attitude of the institution as a whole, saying, "Let us enjoy the papacy, since God has given it to us."[82]

As the hierarchy enjoyed the papacy, the priesthood held ultimate power over the means of grace through the exercise of the mass. The mass, understood as a sacrifice, claimed that the church was constituted by the action of the priest. The community's presence and participation became dispensable. Once this occurred, presence at the mass could be replaced with a financial contribution. This led to the destruction of grace as well as the loss of faithful security and confidence in God. Since the traffic in indulgences provided the immediate cause of the Reformation movement and provides a concrete case of the cooption of grace, it deserves examination.

The church created indulgences in the eleventh century as a means of raising revenues to finance the crusades. So from the beginning violence lurks in the shadows of indulgence sales. The indulgences functioned within the larger penitential system of the church that Luther experienced as another form of violence; this system attacked his soul with throes of insecurity creating tremendous anxiety before the de-

---

81. Böckmann, "Der gemeine Mann in den Flugschriften der Reformation," 187, cited in Blickle, *Communal Reformation*, 118.

82. Cited in Grimm, *Reformation Era*, 38.

mands of God and the church. When Luther's parishioners slipped over the border into Albrecht's territories to buy indulgences, Luther rebelled, writing his famous *Ninety-five Theses*.

Officially, indulgences fit within the sacrament of penance and consisted of three parts: contrition, confession/absolution, satisfaction. Indulgences functioned within the third part of this movement. They took on the burden of the temporal punishments that the church laid upon the penitent for the remission of his or her sins. This pious practice quickly became a business of great import for the church's financial security. Bernhard Lohse writes:

> The practice of selling indulgences was of immense significance for the financial structure of the church. Indulgences were one of the major sources of the income that the papal state required to meet its strong need for money and to finance the many wars in which the papacy was involved. The curia also needed the income from the sale of indulgences to finance its luxurious life style.[83]

The economic interests central to these indulgences are blatant in the official "Summary Instruction" issued to the sellers. After describing the grace that accompanies the purchased indulgence, the confessors are instructed to turn to the economic question. They are officially instructed:

> Concerning the contribution to the chest, for the building of the church of the chief of the apostles, the penitentiaries and confessors are to ask those making confession, after having explained the full forgiveness and privilege of this indulgence: How much money or other temporal goods they would conscientiously give for such full forgiveness? This is to be done in order that afterwards they may be brought all the more easily to make a contribution.[84]

The particular indulgences that Luther encountered created revenue for Albrecht of Brandenburg. He had fees to pay for receiving the Archdiocese of Mainz and for dispensations on the illegal holding of this office. The loan for this payment came from the Fuggers; indulgence profits were earmarked for repayment of this loan.

83. Lohse, *Martin Luther*, 43.
84. Hillerbrand, *Reformation*, 38–39.

The church that provided the means for alleviating troubled souls was the same institution that created that trouble in the souls in the first place. This could be heard as one of the officers in charge of sales, John Tetzel, made his pitch to perspective buyers. Also noteworthy is that the purchase no longer took care of merely temporal punishments, but eternal ones. The infamous Tetzel proclaimed:

> Why are you standing there? Run for the salvation of your souls! Be as careful and concerned for the salvation of your souls as you are for your temporal goods, which you seek both day and night. Seek the Lord while he may be found and while he is near. Work, as St John says, while it is yet day, for the night comes when no man can work. Don't you hear the voices of your wailing dead parents and others who say, 'Have mercy upon me, have mercy upon me, because we are in severe punishment and pain. From this you could redeem us with a small alms and yet you do not want to do so.' Open your hearts as the father says to the son and the mother to the daughter . . . , 'We have created you, fed you, cared for you, and left you our temporal goods. Why then are you so cruel and harsh that you do not want to save us . . . ?[85]

Tetzel used the immense guilt present over the abandonment of parents and loved ones claimed by the plague for utter spiritual, psychological, and financial manipulation. According to the papal instructions, sermons on indulgences were to interrupt and supersede the normal proclamation in Albrecht's territory in order to further the sales.[86] Indulgences, in those territories where the authorities tolerated or supported them, were but a sign of the way the church hierarchy related to the laity. This traffic in salvation is but one example of the exploiting of the peoples' needs, anxieties, and pocketbooks to serve the luxurious life of the church officials. Yet they were also abusing another kind of power.

The world in which the Reformation took shape was charged with an awareness of spiritual powers, both benevolent and malignant, in the affairs of daily life. Heiko Oberman has called attention to this reality in his interpretive biography, *Luther: Man between God and the Devil.*[87] He has exhorted us to recall what modernity has forgotten. Luther lived in

85. Hillerbrand, *Reformation*, 42–43.
86. Brecht, *Martin Luther*, 180.
87. Oberman, *Luther*, 61–64, 209–25.

a time when the devil, God, angels, and demons were not seen as mere metaphors, but were believed to be concrete and active at every place and every time. Luther claimed that indulgences and general church corruption showed the institution's alignment not only with princes and bankers, but also with that prince of darkness, Satan. The leadership of the church had turned its back on the gracious power of God to serve the kingdom of another. The leaders had effectively cut the people off from the gracious gift of God known in Christ Jesus.

As in many moments in history, when the leaders of the church failed the laity, the people found other expressions of faith that did not require the clergy in any significant way.[88] Faced with a church liturgical practice that put the community of the faithful at the margins of sacred activity and that collected monetary fees for the gifts of God, with the higher clergy more and more removed from German, let alone popular, culture, the common people found ways to express their own sense of connectedness with God, with the holy and with each other. Group devotions developed centered on the Blessed Virgin, the Rosary, or the sufferings of Christ. Even at those events that had clergy present, such as a Eucharistic or other procession, "the control of the event slips from the grasp of the clergy and passes over to the people."[89] Through these events and actions, as well as the dispositions that underlay them, the people took seriously their own participation in the sacred, bringing their own popular cultural heritage with them. The line separating the sacred from the profane, the priestly work from the work of the people, and the Roman culture from the German was removed through popular, communal activity and ways of being in the world. The fabric of life was stitched back together to form one whole cloth.

This dynamic from within the popular community expressed in popular religious practices was a way of resisting and protesting against the activities of others who marginalized them. This popular protest was at once social and religious since the life that the people knew was one organic whole. Life was simultaneously social and religious because much of what threatened the people had both of these dimensions. The church as an institution was not simply religious, but also politically and economically active in that context; from the perspective of the

---

88. Scribner, *German Reformation*, 12.

89. Steven-Arroyo and Díaz-Stevens, *An Enduring Flame*, 11.

poor, the church's interests and practices stood closely united with the interests of others who oppressed them. Throughout the Reformation era the convergence of social and religious protest, in whatever form it might have taken, was neither unusual nor irrational. Neither religious nor social dynamics should overshadow one another. Both were integrally related in the mind and life of the people. In fact, the people did not unite two separate elements, but rather our modern interpretations have dis-membered the whole, have separated a unity. Often in theological appraisal of this conjunction of concerns, particularly when done from a strong confessional perspective, interpreters have belittled the popular rationality by claiming that it misunderstood Luther's insights or that it allowed base interests to overshadow the true evangelical message. Blickle writes perceptively:

> forms of social protest have been discredited to the point where the 'common man' is derided as having had 'lower' motives for action in cases where he did participate in introducing the Reformation. This view has even been stylized into a theorem, which is supported by the prescholarly conviction that the 'common man' misunderstood the reformers' intention.[90]

Blickle joins Oberman in the assertion that social protest "can claim its place in church history with the same right as the movements coming out of Wittenberg, Geneva or Trent."[91]

Luther's critique of power, and particularly of ecclesiastical power, was not an abstract, detached critique of the generic operations of human potentiality, but rather a critique embedded in a complex economic, political, social, and religious matrix of power. Though the mapping of each kind of power displays characteristics particular to their own spheres of activity, multiple layers of power concentrated in certain groups, key among them the representatives of the institutional church. Conversely, the vast majority of the people in sixteenth-century Germany were excluded from public power. The church and other powerful institutions of its day often joined hands for the purpose of exploitation. In such a context, religious critique is implicitly and often explicitly social critique. Intense intellectual searching and

90. Blickle, "Social Protest and Reformation Theology," 16.

91. Oberman, "Gospel of Social Unrest," 50, cited and discussed in Blickle, *Revolution of 1525*, 16.

questioning on the part of many groups within society occurred during this period. This offered a window of opportunity in which Luther provided a new field of discourse for the ordering of society. Luther's early writing so spoke to the marginalized people of his day that their hopes for transformation were aroused. How did Luther's theology of the cross insert itself within these gross imbalances of power and the resulting abuse?

3

Luther's Theology of the Cross in Latin

THE WRITINGS OF THE REFORMATION INSERTED THEMSELVES IN THE complex matrix of power of the sixteenth century. While none of these writings is divorced from this reality, all do not enter it by the same doorway. One of the choices Luther had to make in terms of the effect of any given writing within and upon the power structure was the language in which he would communicate. From the first word of a text, Luther had to decide if he was writing for a small minority of those who read and speak Latin, for a larger group of those who read German or at least understood it when it was read aloud, or if he would join hands with a pamphlet artist and attempt more direct communication with all the estates of his country from the lowest to the highest. With the choice of language comes a choice of audience. In the case of the theology of the cross that at heart is always of critique of real imbalances and abuses of power, the shift in linguistic field also indicates a shift in intended audiences and in the power possessed by those who are engaged. The Latin texts that are examined in this chapter were originally intended for debate among the religious elite. The challenge they raised was not primarily to the general community but to those who were power-laden in society. While these texts were quickly translated into German, Luther wrote them with the Latin-speaking religious elite in mind. This audience forms part of the interpretive domain that demands exploration.

Ninety-five Theses

The first important spark of the Reformation, the *Ninety-five Theses,* flew out of a scholarly disputation among learned theologians. This audience was the only one that Luther had imagined would be interested in this debate. He was, of course, wrong; the theses were quickly translated into German and gained a widespread hearing and approval among the German people. Hans Hillerbrand confesses scholarly amazement at the broad impact that these articles made:

> Indeed, it is still one of the mysteries of Reformation history how this proposal for academic disputation, written in Latin, could have kindled such enthusiastic support and thereby have such far-reaching impact. The answer, if there is one, is that Luther had gotten into an ecclesiastical hornet's nest in which there was more than theology involved—prestige and money.[1]

The preoccupations Luther directed at the ecclesiastical leadership also represented concerns that had practical implications for the general populace. The *Ninety-five Theses* grew not only out of Luther's scholarly work, but primarily out of pastoral concern over the exploitation of his parishioners by the indulgence hawkers.[2] Luther even presents some of the theses as arguments that had come to him through "the shrewd questions of the laity."[3] Yet this broad interest must not obscure the fact that Luther wrote for his fellow, ecclesiastical elite. Luther scolds them and the institution that they serve. The translation into Germany was so popular because it transformed a relatively private reprimand into a public scolding.

The opening thesis sets the tone for all that follows. Luther argues: "When our Lord and Master Jesus Christ said, 'Repent' (Matt 4:17), he willed the entire life of believers to be one of repentance."[4] This thesis is the foundation for the reappraisal of the entire penitential system that had evolved into the practice of indulgences. It demands that the church be related to the whole existence of believers, and not only to their pocketbooks as it is when the church accepts indulgence payments as signs of repentance. Luther calls for believers to turn their lives around according to the word and will of God. Yet by calling for a radical, biblically understood repentance, Luther's word challenges much more than the individual believer's life. This introductory thesis could also be understood as the first clue that Luther is calling for the repentance of his specific, intended audience. Luther demands that the

1. Hillerbrand, *Reformation*, 32.
2. Lindberg, *European Reformations*, 72.
3. See Theses 82–90, LW 31:32–33; WA 1.227–28.
4. LW 31.25; WA 1.233.

religious leadership lead the institutional repentance of a guilty church. Not only individual lay believers, but in a special way the institutional leadership are called to "a transition from one state of mind to another, . . . a change of spirit."[5] In the *Explanations*, when Luther specifies whom he is thinking of in this thesis, he says that it applies "to all people, that is, to all people in every walk of life." Yet when he gets specific, he does not even mention the common lay people, but only religious and political leaders: the king, the priest, the princes, the monk, and the mendicant. Luther's call to repentance, while undoubtedly global in intent, is most intensely aimed at those who possessed concentrations of power within the context of the sixteenth century. They, "like Daniel in Babylon," should repent.[6] The Babylonian captivity is already becoming for Luther a metaphor of his society and church's condition. Throughout the theses, the importance of institutional transformation asserts itself in Luther's accusations.

Certainly this thrust was not lost on the original readers, neither those sympathetic with Luther's accusations, nor those most pointedly challenged. His claim that all should repent does not attack each person with equal ferocity. The powerful will feel his challenge more acutely than the rest of the population. This call to repentance relates directly to the theology of the cross. Later in his explanations of these theses, Luther makes the link between the two explicit: ". . . all life is repentance and a cross of Christ." Thus the theologian of the cross will be interested in the "cross of repentance."[7]

The theses that follow critique the ideology of the indulgence hawkers. Luther's attack is two-fold. Firstly, satisfaction is not made before God on the basis of monetary payments to the church. In fact, the church has no right to impose any kind of satisfaction. The final stage of penance is simply the new life that God requires. Luther cites Micah 6 to flesh out what the Lord demands: "and what does the Lord require of you but to do justice, and to love kindness, and to walk humbly with your God."[8] This theme will be picked up in the middle of the treatise. Secondly, Luther calls for the proper limitation of papal powers.

5. LW 31.84; WA 1.531.
6. Ibid.
7. Trans. altered, LW 31.89; WA 1.533–34.
8. LW 31.96; WA 1.538.

Punishment for sins is not in the hands of the pope, but in God's hands. Over and over again, Luther declares the limits to papal jurisdiction with the common refrain that a particular form of authority "is beyond the power of popes."[9] Luther speaks as though he is certain that the pope would agree with him on this point. Whether this is a sincere belief or a rhetorical ploy is not clear. Soon Luther will learn in no uncertain terms that restricting papal powers will not earn him any friends in Rome.

Another blow Luther strikes is against the snare of guilt that Tetzel had laid in his preaching. Luther silences the clamoring voices of the dearly departed whom Tetzel invoked. The dead have no need to cry out from purgatory and indulgences offer them no support. Thus Luther undermines the spiritual and psychological pitch of indulgences sold for the sake of the dead. Luther challenges the ditties of the indulgence hawkers in theses 27 and 28:

> 27. They preach only human doctrines who say that as soon as the money clinks into the money chest, the soul flies out of purgatory.

> 28. It is certain that when money clinks in the money chest, greed and avarice can be increased; but when the church inter-cedes, the result still is in the will of God alone.[10]

Luther here is challenging the hawker's understanding of God. God does not extract payment from the faithful for grace. This would cheapen the gift offered. Luther sinks his dagger in deep in the explanation when he asks about the nature of the God these sellers of salvation serve:

> I do not know whether or not those who speak in such a man-ner want to make God a usurer or merchant, one who remits nothing to us gratis but who expects us to make a satisfaction as payment for the remission.[11]

To make of God a usurer is to Luther the worst way of taking God's name in vain. Luther numbers usurers among murderers and other notorious criminals as the scum of the earth. God is the complete opposite of this usurious idol proclaimed in indulgence sermons. The true God comes in the compassionate Christ claiming, "Any true Christian, whether liv-

9. LW 31.91; WA 1.535.
10. Trans. altered, LW 31.27–28; WA 1.234.
11. Trans. altered, LW 31.117; WA 1.550.

ing or dead, participates in all the goods of Christ and the church; and this is granted him by God, even without indulgence letters."[12]

Luther calls for a refocusing of the church leadership's interest from wealth and buildings financed through indulgences to those people whom God loves. Luther uses strong language. His opponents are "enemies of Christ."[13] Imagine the shock of those selling indulgences to hear this title applied to them. Certainly, the enemies of Christ and his cross are the Turks. Wars against these "enemies of the cross" had been financed through the very sale of indulgences. Suddenly, Luther has reversed the appraisal of who is truly the enemy.

The theses that form the center of this document awakened a cry of support throughout German lands. The attraction to those exploited by the church and, especially to the poor, should be self-evident as we read the theses.

> 42. Christians are to be taught that the pope does not intend that the buying of indulgences should in any way be compared with works of mercy.

> 43. Christians are to be taught that he who gives to the poor or lends to the needy does a better deed than the one who buys indulgences.

> 45. Christians are to be taught that the who sees the needy and passes that one by, yet gives his money for indulgences, does not buy papal indulgences but God's wrath.[14]

A whiff of the nationalist frustration at the cost to Germany of its funds flowing to Rome arises:

> 50. Christians are to be taught that if the pope knew the exactions of the indulgence preachers, he would rather that the basilica of St. Peter were burned to ashes than built up with the skin, flesh and bones of his sheep.

> 51. Christians are to be taught that the pope would and should wish to give of his own money, even though he had to sell the basilica of St. Peter, to many of those from whom certain hawkers of indulgences cajole money.[15]

12. Trans. altered, LW 31.29; WA 1.235.

13. LW 31.30; WA 1.236.

14. LW 31.29; WA 1.235.

15. LW 31.30; WA 1.235.

That theme that launched the *Ninety-five Theses*, the "repentance of the cross," is clearly directed most pointedly at the "hawkers," but perhaps here even to the pope himself. Not St. Peter's basilica or any other edifice in Rome, let alone the corrupt acquisition of the bishopric by Albrecht or the loans flowing to the Fuggers' accounts, are to be the recipients of the alms of the faithful, but rather the poor are to be taken care of in God's name. Luther, in his call to the church to repent, seeks a reversal in which the first become last and the last first.[16]

Luther has raised issues that interested the people of his parish; he makes this explicit beginning with thesis 81. In the next eight theses, Luther purports to relinquish his own voice in order to raise the concerns not of the great scholastic luminaries, but of those whose voices do not normally receive a hearing in academic debates. As in the pamphlet literature discussed earlier, the simple wisdom of the people asks "shrewd questions"[17] with "sharp arguments"[18] that shame the wisdom of the learned. Luther pleads that these concerns be resolved by reason and not "force alone."[19] The citations from the people that Luther provides have to do with their financial and spiritual exploitation by the institutional church. Luther raises up the lowly so that they might ask their pointed questions of the highest levels of the church. Luther has them asking:

> 86. Again, "Why does not the pope, whose wealth is today greater than the wealth of the richest Crassus, build this one basilica of St. Peter with his own money rather than with the money of poor who believe?"[20]

With the voice of the poor, Luther has critiqued the highest authority in the church. While Luther tries to establish some distance from these sharp barbs by claiming they are what he has heard and not necessarily what he himself holds, this distance will soon be eliminated when papal force and not reason come out against Luther.

When, at the request of Albert of Hohenzollern, the theologians of the University of Mainz made their formal assessment of the *Ninety-five*

16. See Theses 63 and 64. LW 31.31; WA 1.236.

17. LW 31.32; WA 1.237.

18. LW 31.33; WA 1.238.

19. LW 31.33; WA 1.238.

20. Trans. altered, LW 31.33; WA 1.237.

Theses, their criticism reveals that they saw Luther's understanding of power as the heart of the problem with his theology. Their reply bears their strongest complaint against Luther's theses, "We have read them and among other things we find that they limit and restrict the power of the Pope and the apostolic see and contradict, therefore, the opinions of many blessed and venerable doctors."[21] This for them is the theological issue. The pope's power is the foundation for ecclesial existence. But obviously the issues are not simply theological. They are bound up in the whole ecclesial project of Rome that far exceeds strictly religious endeavors. Having attempted to reconfigure the understanding of power relationships, Luther is about to experience the brutality that powerful Rome wields with a vengeance.

The critique of concrete, historic power relationships lies at the heart of this early expression by the theology of the cross. When Luther levels his critique of the human use of power, he is not simply concerned with the generic operation of power by all human beings, but with the specific configurations and uses of power within his own context and especially the abuses of the ecclesial leadership. The theology of the cross did not take shape for Luther simply on the basis of his personal crisis, but rather took place in a debate about the proper use of power in the public sphere. Jos Vercruysse offers the correct judgment in this regard when he appropriately insists,

> The theology of the cross, however, is not restricted to the area of personal faith. Luther, as a matter of fact, has elaborated it most explicitly in the context of the matter of indulgences. This link shows its potential for criticism of Christian and ecclesiastical life.[22]

Given the economic, political, and social embeddedness of the church, this criticism addresses not only religious dimensions of the church's institutional life. Luther critiques the whole life of the theologians who debate with him. He calls on them to be theologians of the cross.

Luther explicitly evokes the language of the theologian of the cross in his later *Explanations*. In the explanation of thesis 58, right before the thesis where Luther asserts that the poor are the treasures of the church,

---

21. Hillerbrand, *Reformation*, 52–53.
22. Vercruysse, "Luther's Theology of the Cross," 9.

Luther sets up his contrast between two ways of being a theologian. He writes:

> From this [the call to take up crosses] you can now see how, ever since the scholastic theology—the deceiving theology (for that is the meaning of the word in Greek)—began, the theology of the cross has been abrogated, and everything has been completely turned up-side-down. A theologian of the cross (that is, one who speaks of the crucified and hidden God), teaches that punishments, crosses, and death are the most precious treasury of all and the most sacred relics which the Lord of this theology himself has consecrated and blessed, not alone by the touch of his most holy flesh but also by the embrace of his exceedingly holy and divine will, and he has left these relics here to be kissed, sought after, and embraced.[23]

Luther calls for things to be "turned up-side-down" so that God's will might stand. Luther continues:

> . . . the theologian of glory still receives money for his treasury, while the theologian of the cross, on the other hand, offers the merits of Christ freely. Yet people do not consider the theologian of the cross worthy of consideration, but finally even persecute him.
>
> But who will be the judge of these two, in order that we may know which one to listen to? Behold, Isaiah says, chapter 66 [:4], "I will choose what they ridicule." And I Cor. 1 [:27] states, "God chose what is weak in the world to shame the strong, etc."[24]

These explanations employ the signature language of Luther's theology in order to drive home the themes Luther developed. The theology of the cross takes shape in an atmosphere where the greed of the church makes God out to be a usurer. Luther proposes a radically different understanding of God as one who is concerned first and foremost for the needs of the poor who are at the mercy of the powerful profit mongers. This God does not side with the powerful, but rather chooses the weak to shame the strong. The concern for the gospel blurs into the concern for the exploited and neglected poor because the sheer giftedness of the gospel is not proclaimed in a void. Rather the utter graciousness of God becomes concrete by contrast to the usurious

23. LW 31.225; WA 1.613.
24. LW 31.227; WA 1.614.

and exploitative systems in which the institutional church participates. Luther decries a self-secure church that proclaims only the illusion of peace; he counters the church's diversion tactic with the claim that the only way to be moved beyond the horror of the cross is to speak openly and prophetically of its reality. The turning of repentance is a turning from the illusion of peace to name the real results of the abuse of power as they are manifest in the cross. Theses 92 and 93 put these alternatives in sharp distinctions:

> 92. Away then with all those prophets who say to the people of Christ, "Peace, peace," and there is no peace! [Jer 6:14]

> 93. Blessed be all those prophets who say to the people of Christ, "Cross, cross," and there is no cross.[25]

The church leadership is not to parrot the words of peace where peace does not exist. Rather when no one speaks of the cross that the poor have suffered, the prophet must speak the truth. The crosses erected on the edges of that peaceful kingdom are the sign that the church has been unfaithful; the edges reveal the frailty of the whole. Luther challenges those who have made the world thus. His word is aimed at them. Only later through translation does Luther's scolding of the leadership become public; then the German people rejoice that a voice finally has spoken on their behalf.

Heidelberg Disputation

Several months after the writing of the *Ninety-five Theses*, Martin Luther received an invitation from Johannes von Staupitz to preside over a public disputation of the Augustinians at Heidelberg. Since Luther had already been draw into controversy over the *Ninety-five Theses*, Luther was warned to let the theme of indulgences lie. While he obediently made no explicit references to them, the issues raised in those earlier theses lurked in the shadows at every point.[26] Staupitz asked Luther to address the issues of sin, free will, and grace.[27] In order to address these themes Luther used a strong thesis/antithesis style that held up clear contrasts between two ways of both being in the world and doing theol-

25. LW 31.33; WA 1.238.
26. Brendler, *Martin Luther*, 122.
27. Introduction to the *Heidelberg Disputation*, LW 31.37.

ogy. In the midst of his own reformulating of the nature of the Christian faith, Luther presented his order with the radical theology of the cross.

While contemporary theologians who are interested in the theology of the cross have often rushed to theses 19–22 as their point of departure, they must be careful. For while those theses provide a provocative description of the revelation of God, they do so, within Luther's thought, upon the specific anthropological description that has preceded them. Forde had warned about the danger of this quick leap:

> Unfortunately what usually happens then is that these theses [19–24] are taken out of their context in the Disputation and treated as though they were to stand by themselves as a more or less discrete theological program or treatise on the knowledge of God according to the theology of the cross and such matters.[28]

While Forde is right on this point, it is also true that the first eighteen theses need to be understood as setting up those key theses. What is more, the whole *Disputation* flows out of the controversies that surrounded the *Ninety-five Theses* and its attack on the unjust practices of the church. While Luther obeyed the request to abandon the topic of indulgences, this vow of obedience need not reign over his present-day interpreters.

The *Disputation* has three parts that correspond to the issues that Staupitz wished to have addressed:

1. Sin: Theses 1 to 12

2. Free will or the lack thereof: Theses 13 to 18

3. Grace: Theses 19 to 28

Those theses that address sin and the will are a devastating critique of human quests for righteousness and of human attempts to perceive the works of God. The first theses again lay the groundwork:

1. The law of God, the most wholesome knowledge of life, cannot progress one toward righteousness, but rather is increasingly in the way.

2. Much less are human works, that is, those assisted repeatedly by natural precepts, able to progress one toward righteousness.[29]

28. Forde, *On Being a Theologian of the Cross*, 69.
29. Trans. mine, cf. LW 31.39; WA 1.353.15–18.

The law of God—which Luther not only calls "the most wholesome knowledge of life," but also "holy and immaculate, true and just"—cannot aid mortals in their quest for righteousness. How much less then is human nature on its own able to progress. Three times in the first two theses and their explanations, Luther specifically condemns the illusions of human "progress."[30] In fact, not progress but its contrary is the normal fruit of human endeavor. Luther argues that when there is trust in one's own power, "evil is done increasingly."[31] Luther begins to offer a strong critique of the reigning theological understanding wherein God only requires that people "do what is within them."[32] Though he will not use that specific, scholastic phrase until thesis 13, he introduces the topic by speaking of the tragic result of being "left to one's own powers" or of when "one works out of one's own self."[33] It is in the act of "doing your best"[34] that one most clearly sins, argues Luther. This flies in the face of the way that human beings normally see or interpret reality.

Here Luther launches a critique on the foundations of theology and all of public life in his day. He attacks the law that is not simply a spiritual dynamic that relates to the conscience of the individual, but is the basis for jurisprudence in all realms of life. Within both church and empire, the law functions as the ground for all efforts at understanding, discerning, judging, and legislating. The one-time law student Luther has begun to invite the theologians in front of him to abandon their penchant for defining reality along legal lines. He is dismantling the basis for the old epistemology before articulating the new one.

In the next set of theses Luther lays out in parallel form the contradictions between the human perspective of reality and God's.

  3. The works of humans appear as though they are always beautiful and good; however, it is probable that they are mortal sins.

  4. The works of God appear as though they are always ugly and evil; however, truly they are immortal merits.[35]

---

30. Cf. LW 31.42–43; WA 1.355.31–356.7, 11.

31. Trans. mine, cf. LW 31.43; WA 1.356.10.

32. Trans. mine, cf. LW 31.43; WA 1.356.10–12.

33. Trans. mine, cf. LW 31.43; WA 1.356.10–12.

34. Lindberg's translation of *facere quod in se est*, in *European Reformations*, 67.

35. Trans. mine, cf. LW 31.39; WA 1.353.17–20.

These two theses are set up to play off of each other. Human works stand against divine work; humans appraise good and evil in the opposite way that God does. The consistent structure serves to highlight the radical reversal in the way that God perceives things. The final contrast of "mortal sins" (*peccata mortalia*) and "immortal merit" (*merita immortalia*) drives home the difference. Human acts lead to mortal or deadly sins while the works of God lead to immortal or eternal merit. The human works are mortal sins because they throw people back upon themselves rather than upon God. God's works appear ugly because they humiliate and terrify through the law. Yet they only humiliate in order that humans might confess that they are "nothing, foolish, evil" before God. This divine assault is God's "strange work," which prepares for the work of salvation, God's truest, "characteristic work." Through the law God humbles so that God might exalt. Thus, the Christian is to live not trusting in his or her own powers; rather "we live in the hiddenness of God (that is, in the naked trust in his mercy)."[36]

To trust in God in spite of all appearance to the contrary is to know and confess oneself as "nothing, foolish, evil" without God. Without such an acknowledgement, we trust in our own work for security. Luther writes about such trust:

> to trust in the work, of which one must fear, is to take away the glory from God—who should be feared in every work—and give it to oneself. However this is totally perverse, done no doubt to please oneself and enjoy oneself in one's works and to worship the idol, oneself. However, thus the one who is secure and without fear of God acts in all things.[37]

The quest for self-security, meaning security based on the self in order to serve oneself, leads one only to seek to "please" and "enjoy oneself." This robs God of the divine glory, claiming it for oneself. The glory of God, as Luther defines it here and elsewhere, is the glory of saving human beings. When humans claim to move toward God through their own works, they are guilty of sin. Thus, especially good works, since these most persuasively tempt people to place trust in themselves, are sin. This Luther makes clear in the seventh thesis: "7. The works of the

---

36. Trans. mine, cf. LW 31.44; WA 1.357.3. LW has improperly translated *vivimus in abscondito Dei* as "our life is hidden in God."

37. Trans. mine, cf. LW 31.46; WA 1.358.4–9.

righteous would be mortal sins, except when they would be feared as mortal sins with a pious fear of God by the righteous themselves."[38]

Without such fear, pride reigns. And "God certainly resists the proud; indeed if pride should cease, there also would be no sin anywhere."[39] The proud do not live "in naked trust in [God's] mercy" but rather "in trust in creatures."[40] Recognizing the sinfulness of human works creates a place for faith. When the proud are turned from their "excusing excuses" (*excusandas excusationes*)[41] to honest confession, God's justifying takes place. Or as Luther puts it, "to the extent that we accuse [*accusamus*] ourselves, to that extent God forgives [*excusat*]."[42] Again by excusing themselves, the proud rob God of divine glory; they rob God of the glory of forgiving (*excusando*) them. In this first section sin has been understood as trust in creaturely works, especially "good" works. Luther now turns to the issue of the human will.

The thirteenth thesis leaves no question that Luther's denial of the free will is as robust as his claim that trust in good works equals sin. He writes: "13. After sin [entered the world], the free will is a reality in name alone, and so long as it does what is in it, it sins mortally."[43] The will is by no means free; the will is "captive and enslaved by sin."[44] If one were to speak of freedom, the will is free only to do that which is evil. To progress toward the good is no longer within its own powers. Thus Luther introduces the theme that he will pound out again and again in the following theses. The will cannot be free. If it is not subject to God, then it is enslaved in service to another lord. But when one recognizes that God offers to set the human will free in service to divine will, then hope can be born. Quoting Hosea 13, Luther argues in chiastic form: Your lostness [comes] from you, Israel. From me—only me alone—[comes] your help.[45] The structure sets up the contrasts nicely. Trust in what comes from you and you get lostness; trust in what comes from God alone and you get help. The flow is only interrupted for the sake of defi-

38. Trans. mine, cf. LW 31.40; WA 1.353.27.

39. Trans. mine, cf. LW 31.47; WA 1.358.32.

40. Trans. mine, cf. LW 31.48; WA 1.359.25.

41. Trans. mine, cf. LW 31.48; WA 1.359.31.

42. Trans. mine, cf. LW 31.48; WA 1.359.29–30.

43. Trans. mine, cf. LW 31.40; WA 1.354.5–6.

44. Trans. mine, cf. LW 31.48; WA 1.359.35.

45. Trans. mine, cf. LW 31.49; WA 1.360.3–4.

nite emphasis with "only me alone." Though the will is bound, God is capable of taking hold of it and transforming it in Christ. "Now the free will is dead, meaning by dead those whom the Lord has raised."[46] The state of enslavement is compounded when this reality is denied. On the one hand, one is guilty for doing evil; on the other, one is again guilty for believing that this is not evil but good. Luther accuses such people of believing that "sin is not sin and evil is not evil."[47] Luther's specific meaning here matters; later in thesis 21 he uses the same vocabulary again. Luther is critiquing the specific scholastic notion that all God requires of mortals is that they "do what is within them." Luther snorts emphatically at the scholastics, saying "we do nothing that is not sin."[48]

So what hope can there be? If one lives by the law, trusting in one's own will, no hope is possible. The law only makes human beings "take note of sin." It "works fear and wrath." But the grace of God gives life to the humble:

> Thus [God] gives grace to the humble, and whoever is humbled, is exalted. The law humbles, grace exalts. The law works fear and wrath, grace works hope and mercy. Through the law, knowledge of sin is acquired; through the knowledge of sin, moreover, humility is acquired; through humility, grace is acquired. Thus a strange work of God leads at last to God's characteristic work: God makes one a sinner in order to make the same just.[49]

The grace of God leads "at last"—the sinners sighs—to salvation. Thus to confess oneself a sinner is not "to give cause for despairing, but rather for humbling oneself, and to inspire an eagerness for seeking the grace of Christ." Luther explains that this must be so, "since according to the gospel, children and the poor shall be given the kingdom of heaven and Christ loves them."[50] Thus this section closes with the plea not to trust in one's own "strength," but to "utterly despair of one's own ability so that one might be made fit for the consequent grace of Christ."[51] The

46. Trans. mine, cf. LW 31.49; WA 1.360.9–10.
47. Trans. mine, cf. LW 31.50; WA 1.360.29–30.
48. Trans. mine, cf. LW 31.50; WA 1.360.34–35.
49. Trans. mine, cf. LW 31.50–51; WA 1.360.38–361.5.
50. Trans. mine, cf. LW 31.51; WA 1.361.9–10.
51. Trans. mine, cf. LW 31.51; WA 1.361.23–24.

law "makes one poor"[52] in preparation for grace. Thus ends the section on the lack of free will.

This scathing critique of human power and of the illusion of progress needs to be understood in light of the specific critique of theologians that follows. Theologians, after all, heard this disputation and were Luther's intended audience. Luther expounds on the propensity of theologians to turn from suffering in search of glory. In another writing of this period Luther addresses his concern with philosophical study. Loewenich correctly paraphrases Luther's concern with intellectuals who search "into the essences and actions of creatures rather than into their groanings and expectations."[53] This particular critique of the quest for glory and the flight from human suffering by the institutional church and its thinkers interprets the critique of human pretensions that Luther has already expounded. Though Luther has attacked the universal tendency of human beings to usurp the glory of God, this universal critique functions as the foundation for a very specific critique of the reigning theologians and churchmen with their concrete arrogance, their embeddedness in the law as jurisprudence and their economic ambitions. Luther has laid out the limitations of both law and work; these are not merely theological categories. They represent the public realms of law and labor where power is exercised and often abused.[54] As with the call to repentance in the *Ninety-five Theses*, though the critique is offered to all, it is more pointedly and painfully felt by those in power. In fact, as this disputation moves forward out of the momentum of the *Ninety-five Theses* and the controversy over indulgences, Luther's attack continues against the same enemies of the cross. The generic critique of human powers functioned at the same time in a strategic fashion radically challenging power relationships within the community of theological discourse!

Luther challenged the reigning theological discursive field (particularly the law as the reigning basis for epistemology) and its theologians. He robbed them of their legal authority and opened up a space for numerous alternatives to assert themselves. A shifting of the ground occurred through Luther's argument that was specifically threatening

52. Trans. mine, cf. LW 31.51; WA 1.361.26.

53. Loewenich, *Luther's Theology of the Cross*, 69; cf. LW 25.362; WA 16.372–73.

54. Westhelle, *Scandalous God*, 48.

to the scholastic theologians rooted in an international legal system. Luther's concrete attack was against their arsenal. His criticism aimed specifically at their slogans such as "to do what is within you." Even more, these theses are an all out attack on the law as the basis for theological discernment. The scholastic theologians' epistemology is attacked at its point of origin in the law. Many who will not accept the specific alternative that Luther proposes, nonetheless celebrated his breaking open of the discursive field. It was as though all the cards had been held in the hands of a few. When Luther knocked the cards out of their hands, many applauded his audacity before stooping down to pick up the cards and create their own more favorable hands.

The actual content of Luther's anthropology did not lend dramatic assistance to the ideas of many who applauded him. Yet the dynamic challenge thrown at his contemporaries opened a space of legitimacy for other alternative approaches. Luther's act of undermining the old foundation in the law and work and of then proposing a viable alternative offers hope to others who had been searching for different models. Luther brought about radical power shifts in the realm of ideology or interpretation. Those who did not accept his specific doctrinal assertions still appreciated this breaking open of the discursive field. While Luther did hold to the concept of the enslaved will and continued to hold it throughout his life, it was not merely a concept unto itself. It also functioned strategically in his context as an attack on reigning epistemological structures.

The humanist support of Luther illustrates this point well. After hearing this disputation, Bucer spoke enthusiastically of Luther and his supporters, claiming, "They all agree with Erasmus, but one man seemed to stand out, for what he [Erasmus] merely implies, this one [Luther] teaches openly and freely."[55] Certainly Bucer is not speaking of the enslaved will here! Nothing will come to mark the difference between Erasmus and Luther more than this issue. Despite the fact that Luther spends so much of his treatise of the enslaved will, Bucer thinks that this is a curious novelty in the midst of an otherwise excellent dispute.[56] Later in life, Luther explicitly and vehemently denies that he used this concept in a merely tactical fashion. Yet even Luther

---

55. Cited in Moeller, *Imperial Cities and the Reformation*, 26.
56. Ibid., 28.

vehemence shows that the tactical interpretation was widely embraced. Many of the reformers were humanists who never bought into Luther's anthropology wholeheartedly. Even central Lutheran confessional documents demonstrate the difference in perspective between Luther and other reformers. *The Augsburg Confession* has an article titled not "Concerning the Enslaved Will," but "Concerning the Free Will." What is more, even as Luther himself wrote this disputation's scathing attack on the human will, he was signing his correspondence "*Eleutherius*," Greek for the "free one."

All this to say, ideas not only are concepts; they function as elements of the social and intellectual context that may reconfigure power relationships. According to the widespread support Luther received from humanists and others, the generic critique of human potentiality functioned at the same time concretely and particularly as an ideological challenge to scholastic theologians and the institutional church that they supported through their articulation of the law, whether ecclesiastical or imperial. Specifically, Luther challenges those who claim that salvation is not God's gift but is the result of doing what is within one's wallet to procure salvation. We will want to be attentive in our examination of other writings to analogous claims of human enslavement. When Luther moved out of discourse that addressed intellectuals into different forms such as sermons addressed among others to the common people, the understanding of the enslaved will is not a central theme.

When Luther's message moves into more popular media, the assertion of generic human fallenness dissipates. It is almost nonexistent in the pamphlet literature that translated Luther's message with an eye toward the larger population. Cranach's *The Law and the Gospel* portrays such a generic person; yet it is notable mostly as an exception to the rule. It proves that this idea could be portrayed pictorially and so something else must account for its absence in the pamphlet literature. Rather than generic humanity, the pamphlets develop the strategic critique of specific estates in their quest for power and progress at the cost of the rest of the people. Not generic human potentiality, but specific sinful abuses of power suffer Luther's attacks.

We return now to those theses that have aroused the most interest among contemporary theologians and that have proved fertile ground for reflection on how theologians should think about God's presence in the world. As Luther begins to expound upon the section which we have entitled "grace," he talks of two distinctive ways of trying to be a theologian:

> 19. That person does not deserve to be called "theologian" who sees the invisible things of God, in and of themselves, as though they were given to be comprehended in that which happens.
>
> 20. That person [does deserve to be called "theologian"], however, who comprehends the visible things and backside of God seen in suffering and the cross.[57]

To those who desire to know God truly, Luther says, turn from what appears to be beautiful—all that is saturated in glory—toward that which is avoided and despised by the world, the cross and suffering. God is hidden in the cross of Christ and also in the crosses of those who suffer. Luther chastises those who would attend to essences without listening to creaturely groaning. The cross of Christ is the key that allows a person to trust in the gracious presence of God in suffering. There God meets humanity in a way that defies all normal expectations. God is present in "humanity, weakness, foolishness,"[58] as insisted upon in 1 Corinthians. Since humanity abused the knowledge of God known in what is beautiful, God willed to be revealed in suffering. "Thus, it is not sufficient and does no one any good, to know God in glory and majesty, unless that one knows the same in the lowliness and disgrace of the cross."[59]

Both of these locations have a double meaning. On the one hand, the theologian looks toward the lowliness and disgrace of Jesus on the cross rather than toward God in glory and majesty. So this thesis speaks of where God reveals Godself. But, on the other hand, it also speaks of the place *from which* God is seen, that is, the location of the theologian. The theologian of the cross knows God from the place of lowliness and disgrace, rather than from a place of glory and majesty. This place is not a place of sentimentality, but of solidarity. The call to locate oneself among the lowly is held together with the call to see God's presence in the same. This call to the side of the lowly is the means through which "God destroys the wisdom of the wise."[60] Luther proclaims that the best epistemological starting point is the cross. Having opposed the old basis

57. Trans. mine, cf. LW 31.40; WA 1.354.17–20.

58. Trans. mine, cf. LW 31.52; WA 1.362.4–5.

59. Trans. mine, cf. LW 31.52–53; WA 1.362.11–13.

60. LW 31.53; WA 1.13–14.

for epistemology in the law, he proposes an alternative. This epistemological shift is reaffirmed in the twenty-second thesis: "22. That wisdom
which sees the invisible things of God known in works is entirely puffed
up, blinded, and hardened."[61]

The problem with looking for God in glory and majesty is not
merely the threat of error in understanding, though this also exists; rather the problem is that those who see God in glory and power inevitably
seek to establish their own glory and power at the expense of others.
This is precisely what Luther, the one-time law student, has come to see
with utmost clarity. Just as the poor are ignored in the epistemological
pursuits of the theologian of glory, they are marginalized in practice by
the church of such theologians. In the church leadership's upward quest
for God's throne, the poor, weak, and vulnerable are stepped on. Luther
refers to this conjunction of knowledge and power as "*volatilem cogitatum.*"[62] LW translates this as "flighty thought," which, for me, conjures
up images of frivolous, scatterbrained thought. But Luther condemns
"volatile thought," that is, thinking that is prone to erupt into violence.
Not only in the *Disputation*, but throughout Luther's career, this is his
fervent concern about the quest for power and glory.

This concern on Luther's part arises out of his own experience and
observations. He has already felt the force of *volatilem cogitatum* in the
controversy surrounding the *Ninety-five Theses*. Recall the legal verdict
of the University of Mainz: "We find that [Luther's theses] limit and
restrict the power of the Pope and the apostolic see . . ."[63] This verdict
was backed up by the threats of the institutional church and empire.
The violence against Luther's own person and movement only increases
as he approaches the Diet at Worms. Other conjunctions of knowledge,
power, and violence occur in his context. Tetzel is sneered at by Luther
throughout the *Explanations of the Ninety-five Theses* as the "inquisitor"
because of his role in the Inquisition's own particular logic of violence.
Also the systemic violence of usury—this is how Luther saw it—was
buttressed by the legal arguments expounded by Luther's opponent
John Eck. Benjamin Nelson notes that in 1515, "Luther's notorious adversary was making his way to the University of Bologna on behalf of

61. Trans. mine, cf. LW 31.40 WA 1.354.23–24.
62. WA 1.362.16–17; cf. LW 31.53.
63. Hillerbrand, *Reformation*, 52–53.

the Fuggers to prove the legitimacy of the five per cent triple contract."[64] Finally, when Cajetan interrogated Luther at Worms, he was in Germany gathering support from German rulers for concerted military action against the Turks.[65] Luther both intuitively and explicitly sensed this conjunction of discourse and violence. According to Luther, the cross provides a safeguard against reason lapsing into violence. He therefore argues, "In Christ crucified is true theology and knowledge of God."[66]

On the basis of the distinction that Luther draws between the theologians of glory and the theologians of the cross, he notes that not only do theologians of glory seek a glorified God, not only do they seek also their own glory, not only are they prone to erupt in violence, but also they seek to cover this wrongdoing. Thus: "21. A theologian of glory calls evil good and good evil. A theologian of the cross calls the thing what it in fact is."[67]

Of course, Luther is not prophesying here about twentieth-century critical realism as some interpreters use these verses. This thesis hearkens back to thesis 16 where Luther argues that those who deny the enslavement of the will and celebrate human works believe that "sin is not sin, and evil is not evil."[68] The primary evil that Luther is condemning is the sin of claiming that one has freedom without the gift of Christ. Yet, Luther is thinking concretely about sin in the legalized abuse practiced by the institutional church. This is a continuation of his critique of volatile knowledge. He writes in his explanation of the twenty-first thesis:

> It is clear, since the one who is ignorant of Christ, is ignorant of the God hidden in sufferings. Thus that one prefers works to sufferings, glory to cross, power to weakness, wisdom to foolishness, and universally good to evil.[69]

Once again, the direction of the glory-seeking theologian's intellectual pursuit is reflected in their lived preferences, and that universally, Luther insisted. Rather than seek power and glory, one must recognize that God meets and saves the faithful not in glory, but in the suffering

---

64. Nelson, *Idea of Usury*, 25.

65. Hillerbrand, *Reformation*, 35.

66. Trans. mine, cf. LW 31.53; WA 1.362.18–19.

67. Trans. mine, cf. LW 31.40; WA 1.354.21–22.

68. Trans. mine, cf. LW 31.50; WA 1.360.29–30.

69. Trans. mine, cf. LW 31.53; WA 1.362.26–28.

and lowliness of the cross. In the shelter of the cross, the law cannot condemn, but outside of the cross, the law is deadly: "23. The law works the wrath of God, kills, curses, accuses, judges, and damns whoever is not in Christ."[70]

Luther's strong critique of human wisdom in light of the "wisdom of God" manifest on the cross was clearly directed against the reigning, though waning, theological model of his day. The wisdom of the scholastics, according to Luther, did not gaze upon the cross in order to derive their understanding of God. "Who would?" Luther asks. After all, in the cross there is "nothing else to be seen than disgrace, poverty, death and everything that is shown us in the suffering of Christ."[71]

Despite the human flight to that which is beautiful, or maybe even because of it, God has chosen to be revealed in the cross and suffering. Luther does not deny that humans are able to see God present in the world. After all, God is there. Luther contends that when the scholastic theologians opted to see God's presence through a lens other than the cross, they "abused the best in the worst possible manner."[72] A very brief summary of Luther's thought in the disputation thus far is that faith in the Crucified fights against all appearances as they are codified and legislated in what is held to be most clear, glorious, powerful, and worthy. The cross of Christ turns us toward what (and those whom!) we would rather ignore, that which (and those who) in the eyes of world are foolish, undignified, weak, and unworthy of attention.

Together with the two options of theologian of the cross and theologian of glory is the corresponding pair of faith and law. The theologian of the cross sees God's presence in suffering only through the eyes of faith. The theologian of glory looks to the law and human subservience to it for blessings. Such a theologian is bound to be disappointed. For as stated above, the law works wrath; it assumes the role of judge, jury, and witness and thus leads always to condemnation. The law reveals the violence present in the ways of humanity, but offers no release from that spiral of violence. Rather it acts violently on humans. "The law says, 'do this,' and it is never done."[73] Grace, however, brings about what the

70. Trans. mine, cf. LW 31.23; WA 1.354.25–26.
71. WA 5.108.1f, cited in Loewenich, *Luther's Theology of the Cross*, 28.
72. Trans. mine, cf. LW 31.41; WA 1.354.27–28.
73. Trans. mine, cf. LW 31.41; WA 1.354.31–32.

law requires by a totally other means. "Grace says, 'Believe in this,' and everything is already done."[74] By faith, we are in Christ and are made one with him. So another important distinction has asserted itself. Citing Augustine, Luther claims, "The law requires [*imperat*] what faith acquires [*impetrat*]."[75] Not the law, but faith in Christ opens up a whole new world for the believer.

Finally, in the twenty-eighth theological thesis, God's way of acting is presented as a radical alternative to human ways of acting. "God's love does not find, but rather creates, that which is pleasing to it; human love begins in that which is pleasing to it."[76] Human love seeks that which is ready made for enjoyment; the advent of God's love precedes that which it creates, resulting in the transformation of the object of affection. There is a sense where Luther has come full circle to the early theses where he spoke of alternative visions of what is beautiful and what is ugly. There, too, the pattern had been set for two radically different ways of perceiving the world. God's way of being in the world is now laid bare:

> the first part of this thesis is apparent, because the love of God which lives in a human being, highly esteems [*diligit*] sinners, the wretched, fools and the weak in order to make them just, good, wise, empowered; In this way, [the love of God] flows out and yields what is good. Therefore, sinners are beautiful because they are highly esteemed; they are not highly esteemed because they are beautiful. On the contrary, human love flees from sinners and evil. Thus Christ says, "I have not come to call the righteous, but sinners." And this is the love of the cross, born out of the cross, which directs itself not to where it finds good [*bonum*] which might be enjoyed, but to where it may contribute good [*bonum*] to the wretched or destitute. "It is more blessed to give than to receive," says the apostle. And Psalm 41, "Blessed is the one who comprehends the destitute and the poor." For this reason, the object of [the theologian of glory's] comprehension cannot be that which is nothing, that is, the poor or destitute, but only an entity, the true or good. Therefore it judges according to appearances and accepts a person according to their role and judges by what is apparent, etc.[77]

74. Trans. mine, cf. LW 31.41; WA 1.354.31–32.

75. Trans. mine, cf. LW 31.56; WA 1.364.23.

76. Trans. mine, cf. LW 31.41; WA 1.354.35–36.

77. Trans. mine, cf. LW 31.4757–58 WA 1.365.8–20.

This thesis demonstrates the great reversal that the love of God creates. Through the love or esteem of God, sinners become just, the wretched are made good, fools are made wise, and the weak are empowered. God approaches those who seem ugly by human or legal standards, and makes them beautiful. Human comprehension moves to seize that which in and of itself already offers it pleasure. The theologians of glory, that is, those who direct themselves toward glory and power, comprehend things according to their own interests. Luther was accusing the brightest and best of the church's theologians; they have been the ones who used the law to define the meaning of words such as "sinners." They were able to use this to their advantage in their own pursuit of good or profits as the double meaning of *bonum* suggests.

By the end of the theological theses a theme that was hidden below the surface is revealed; in the kind of *intellectus* employed by the theologian of glory, that is, what Luther called volatile knowledge, the poor do not enter the picture. This exclusion is itself a form of violence. For human beings bent on accumulating power, prestige, and profits, the poor "do not exist." The early theses spoke of ugliness that is hated and beauty that is pursued. In the end, it is clear that what is perceived as ugly is not only the cross of Christ, but also the poor and destitute. The whole argument ends with a five-fold invocation of the destitute or poor, and the declaration of blessedness on those who comprehend (*intelligit*) them. This "Blessed is the one who comprehends [*intelligit*] the destitute and poor" reflects the essential, central thesis on the theologian of the cross who "comprehends [*intelligit*] the visible things and backside of God seen in suffering and the cross."[78] The poor and destitute are identified as the backside of God where revelation takes place. The object of faithful *intellectus* is found in suffering of the cross and the poor.

The *theologia crucis* is not finally about the content of theology, but is primarily concerned with how the theologian goes about understanding the things of God. Luther is proposing a way to do theology much more than specific doctrinal concepts. God has revealed Godself in the cross of Christ. This bewilders all human attempts at speculation; it challenges all who take the law as their starting point. Only the faith that looks to the cross is able to see clearly the world and God's relationship to it. The cross is the test of all human wisdom and experience.

78. Trans. mine, cf. LW 31.40; WA 1.354.17–20.

What is more, when looked upon with the eyes of faith, the cross is itself generative of a different kind of wisdom and experience, what might be called an alien experience. First, the cross shatters human delusions of grandeur. In the cross, God "humbles us thoroughly, making us despair."[79] Thus Luther can say that "it is through living, indeed through dying and being damned that one becomes a theologian, not through understanding, reading or speculation."[80] Yet this thorough humbling is for a purpose since "God humbles us thoroughly, making us despair *so that* he may exalt us in his mercy, giving us hope."[81] The suffering that God causes is our most precious treasure. In the cross of Christ, God comes out against humanity in order to establish Godself as unconditionally for humanity. The God who is unknown in speculation becomes revealed in the cross as God for us.

The cross gives the faithful a new world, having shattered the old one. To believe that this world is real is to have all things anew. As Luther often states in his writings, "To the extent that you believe, to that extent do you have."[82] Faith in Christ yields an alternative way of seeing things from the perspective provided by the world. Through the eyes of faith, one receives the whole world anew. Luther has utterly shattered humanity in order to offer the promise of God that restores the believer to a new dignity upon the firm basis in the crucified Christ. Feuerbach was certainly right when he observed, "What Luther takes away from you in your human condition, he replaces for you a hundredfold in God."[83] Without the crucified Christ we are nothing, yet we are not without the crucified Christ and so we are blessed.

Again, the context in which Luther formulated his methodology matters. The valuing of suffering as God's most precious gift was not presented in a vacuum. Nor is it spoken in this case to those who know suffering too well. Luther issued a challenge to a smug, secure church founded in a self-serving legal system; he demanded that the church leadership not flee from suffering—that of Christ or that of humanity. Suffering is the greatest treasure God offers the church. Luther called

79. LW 31.44; WA 1.357.7.

80. WA 5.163.28–29, cited in Lindberg, *European Reformations*, 78.

81. LW 31.44; WA 1.357.7–8.

82. Trans. mine, cf. LW 35.16; WA 2.719.8.

83. Feuerbach, *Essence of Faith According to Luther*, 43.

the church's leadership to hear the suffering cries of the people, and chastised them for their tendency to ignore suffering. Luther's reflections, like those of any theologian, were an attempt to speak to the particular concerns of the day as he perceived them. This disputation and the theology that followed it were directed against a church that had grown haughty in its own security. His leveling of all human wisdom and experience was first and foremost an attack against the scholastic theologians, and, more generally, the papacy. His later emphasis on the freedom of God was formulated over and against the captivity of God and God's gifts in the church of his day. His call to see God's presence in suffering was a challenge to the scholastics who looked to the law rather than to the suffering of the cross to formulate their concept of God. His call to welcome suffering as a treasure was polemically addressed to the church hierarchy that was obsessed with treasures of another sort. Rather the crucified Christ groaning on the cross calls the leadership to stop robbing the people and to pay attention to the people's groanings and expectations.

4

Luther's Theology of the Cross in German

HAVING LOOKED AT THE GENERAL SHAPE OF LUTHER'S THEOLOGY OF the cross in two Latin works, we turn to some of his more devotional, occasional writings that were originally printed in German. While Luther's sharply antithetical language and his attack on the scholastic theologians aroused the interest of the humanists, his devotional writing captured the hearts of the common people.[1] How will themes from the Latin literature appear when presented in this new media? What continuity exists between Luther's Latin disputations and his German reflections? Does Luther in these more popular writings hold to his principle that true theology is in the crucified Christ? What new contours did his confession take on when it was spoke outside of the university to the general public?

The Blessed Sacrament of the Holy and True Body of Christ and the Brotherhoods

In 1519, Luther wrote three sermons to proclaim in simple yet profound form the meaning of the sacraments. By this time Luther's understanding of the sacraments already caused him to write on only three of the seven Roman sacraments: confession and absolution, baptism, and the Lord's Supper. We will look at the third of these sermons in search of continuities as well as new contours in the theology of the cross. This sermon, like the catechisms written a decade later, had as their primary purpose the education of the faithful in the most basic matters of Christian belief.

---

1. Scribner, "Germany," 16.

In Luther's sacramental understanding three elements are present. In the introductory paragraph of the sermon, Luther states what those three things are. The first is the sign. The second is the meaning or significance of the sign in light of God's word of promise. The last is the faith that is necessary to make them effective and useful.

The first element is external and visible. The second element is received within the spirit of the person. Finally, faith unites and empowers the other two elements in order to fulfill the promise given. Faith refers to the way in which the reception of the gifts is made possible. The sign in this sacrament is the eating and drinking of the bread and wine. Both tangible elements and the gesture of consuming them combine to make the sign. The words of Jesus at the time of institution define the significance of the supper. And faith clings to the significance of God's promises as if in the sharing of the sacrament those promises were spoken again directly from heaven. The centrality of faith in Luther's theology is what is most striking and constitutes our first point of contact with the theology of the cross since that theology is always a theology of faith in God and God's grace.

The central element in the practice of this means of grace is faith. Of the three parts of the sacraments, faith alone is ultimately essential. Without faith these gifts are of no use. Yet one does not conjure up this faith on one's own. Even the faith that grasps these gifts is itself a gift from God. Faith is able to trust in the presence and gifts of God in spite of all appearances. "FAITH is that on which its power depends,"[2] states Luther emphatically. This faith does not come easy, for it engages in a "fierce fight."[3]

The significance of the sacrament as Luther identifies it is fresh and challenging on many levels. He states boldly at various times throughout the sermon that ". . . this sacrament means, as we shall see, the complete union and the undivided community of the saints."[4] Luther is already using "saints" in a sense inclusive of all the faithful, both living and dead, as he clarifies in the sermon later by stating "all his saints in heaven and *on earth*."[5]

---

2. Trans. mine, cf. LW 35.60; WA 2.749.30–31.

3. LW 35.60; WA 2.749.36.

4. Trans. mine, cf. LW 35.50; WA 2.742.33.

5. LW 35.53; WA 2.744.28–29 (emphasis mine).

Luther articulates his emphasis on the complete community in a number of ways. He backs up his assertion that the meaning of the sacrament is community with the vocabulary he employs to talk about the sacrament. The controlling or operative set of words in the sermon is "community," "communal," and "common," which share linguistic roots with each other. Within the main body of the sermon (a total of twelve pages in the Weimar edition), that is, excluding the critique of the brotherhoods and the postscript, Luther uses these words seventy-eight times. The anchor word "community" (*Gemeinschaft*) carries the senses of community, shared participation, something held in common like a possession or interest, communion or union with another, partnership, or other related meanings.

In addition to this fundamental vocabulary, other words also rise up to support the sovereignty of his theme. The text is amply seasoned with words invoking the communal ideal like "whole," "full," "one," "all," "union," "unity," and "body." Furthermore, these words are contrasted with other words like "parts" and "divided" that articulate for Luther an unacceptable alternative to the true understanding of the sacrament. His theme is amply reinforced.

Luther uses a variety of words to speak of the oneness that is created. One of his favorite images is the body politic. Using this analogy, Luther notes that the decree that one is a citizen entails both a promise of protection and a call to responsibility. Citizens are bound together in such a way that they, for better or worse, share a common fate. One shares with the other members of the city a "name, honor, freedom, trade, customs, usages, help, support, protection, and the like," and on the other hand, one shares "all the dangers of fire and flood, enemies and death, losses, taxes, and the like."[6] As it is in the body politic, so it is and should be with us in the church.

Luther borrows another image for the sacramental community from St. Paul and then enlivens with his popular imagination. The community is like a human body. He writes:

> if anyone's foot hurts them, yes, even the little toe, the eye at once looks at it, the fingers grasp it, the face puckers, the whole body

6 LW 35.52; WA 2.743.31–34.

> bends over it, and all are concerned with this small member;
> again, once it is cared for all the other members are benefited.[7]

Luther's creativity gives new life and earthiness to this old image bringing it to bear on the common experience of mutuality within the human body. As it is in the human body, so it is and should be with us in Christ's body.

Luther also borrows another image from the received tradition that makes clear that the members of the community are intimately related. Commenting on the sacramental elements, he states:

> For just as the bread is made out of many grains ground and
> mixed together, and out of the bodies of many grains there
> comes the body of one bread, in which each grain loses its form
> and body and takes upon itself the common body of the bread;
> and just as the drops of wine, in losing their own form, become
> the body of one common wine and drink, so it is and should be
> with us.[8]

Still borrowing from the ancient church, Luther comments that the elements are to be consumed. Just as the food eaten becomes one with the human body, so we are to become one with each other. "For there is no more intimate, deep, and indivisible union than the union of the food with the one who is fed. Other unions, achieved by such things as nails, glue, cords and the like, do not make one indivisible substance of the objects joined together."[9] Again, the point: as this is in eating, so it is and should be with us in the church.

The most startling extended use of metaphorical language in this writing could easily be missed by the reader. Consider the title of this sermon: *The Blessed Sacrament of the Holy and True Body of Christ, and the Brotherhoods.* Given the focus in the title on the *Holy and True Body*, one might expect that this sermon would deal with the doctrine of transubstantiation or offer an alternative to that doctrine that still would somehow explain how the elements become the true body of Christ. Yet while Luther at this point in his life still accepts the doctrine of transubstantiation and in this sermon even makes passing reference

7. Trans. altered, LW 35.52; WA 2.744.2–6.

8. LW 35.58; WA 2.748.30–33. An ancient instance of this image is in the second-century *Didache*.

9. Trans. altered, LW 35.59; WA 2.748.29–32.

to it, the true body with which he is obsessed throughout the essay is what he calls the spiritual body, the community of Christ and the faithful. He even takes the explicitly sacramental vocabulary of his time that is meant to speak of the bread and wine becoming Christ's body and blood, and applies it to the way that God creates the community. Listen to the assertion he makes if the sacramental overtones are rendered explicit in the translation:

> For just as the bread is transubstantiated [*vorwandelt*] into his true, natural body and the wine into his natural true blood, thus truly *we* also *are transubstantiated* [*vorwandelt*] and absorbed into the spiritual body which is the community of Christ and all the saints.[10]

While *vorwandelt* also has the ordinary meaning of transformed or changed, Luther is clearly using it in the technical sense. He helps the hearer make the connection by using the word in the strict sacramental sense in the first pair of clauses and then immediately repeating the verb in relation to the transformation of the community. In order to make this connection yet more direct he uses the "just as . . . thus" construction intensified with "also." So that no doubt be left in the reader's mind as to the parallel he is presenting, Luther repeats *wahrhaftig* (translated above as both "true" or "truly") three times, first in terms of the transubstantiated elements and finally in terms of God's transubstantiating of the community.

Luther's claim is intense; God is doing something extremely sacred to the community. Luther vehemently declares in regards to the community what he will later argue with Zwingli in regards to the elements. The community *is* Christ's body. While modern ears might prefer the language of transformation to transubstantiation in relation to the community, *vorwandelt* translated as transubstantiation makes clear that the transformation is God's unambiguous act of truly doing what is promised. In this Luther is claiming that the transforming power of God is not only present in the conscience of the individual, but gains a foothold in history through embodiment in particular communities of faith.

Continuing with the metaphor of transubstantiation, in a later part of the sermon, Luther chastises those who see only the real pres-

---

10. Trans. and emphasis mine, cf. LW 35.59; WA 2.747.23–25.

ence of the body of Christ in the consecrated host, but who are blind
to the fact that what Christ values is his spiritual or sacred body there
created. "For it is more needful that you discern the spiritual [that is,
the holy community] than the natural [that is, in the host] body of
Christ."[11] Luther, unlike later Lutheran orthodoxy, correctly is interpreting St. Paul's comment that "all who eat and drink without discerning
the body, eat and drink judgment against themselves."[12] The body to
which St. Paul is referring is the community of faith. The word that is
translated as "discern" (*acht*) might also be translated as "reverence" or
"venerate." Therefore, by his use of sacramental language he is making
huge claims about the community gathered. It is more important that
we *reverence/venerate* the sacramental community than the sacramental elements. Or, again, not the eucharistic *host*, but the whole *host* of the
faithful on heaven and on earth, is the chief locus of God's activity. This
calls to mind Luther's critique in the *Ninety-five Theses* of those who
revere relics and pilgrimages while neglecting their own family or the
poor in their midst.

Having established the way Luther sets up the meaning of the
sacrament, two questions arise. First, how can this be so? Second, what
does this mean for us? For Luther the community is first and foremost
a gift of God; the community's existence is a result of divine action.
Only in light of the fact that this *is* the case can Luther state what the
community *should* be. Yet even when Luther tells the community what
it should be, his call is not *to* creative human action, but rather is a call
from destructive human actions. The members do not have to be built
into a body, as though building a Frankenstein; God has taken care of
that work. Rather the faithful are to receive the gift of the whole in such
a way as to not deny, dishonor, damage, or dismember the body that
God creates as a gift.

This sermon is surprising on a number of levels. First of all, it must
have been surprising in its own time. Wherein conventional theology
of this sacrament emphasized the power of the priest, Luther expounds
upon the sacrament with only incidental reference to priests. What is
more, Luther does not even use the word "church," which would trigger
images of the institutional church, but rather speaks in terms of com-

---

11. The parenthetical explanations are my own. LW 35.62; WA 2.751.13–15.

12. 1 Corinthians 11:29 (NRSV).

munity. In this way he redefines the essence of church as the gathered community, rather than the hierarchal leadership. The silence in relation to both the priesthood and the institutional church are as radically challenging as the defiant things that Luther actually says. Finally, within an increasingly individualistic eucharistic piety, wherein the benefits are conferred not upon the gathered community, but to the sponsor of the mass, Luther reasserts a biblical understanding of community. The laity is moved from the margins of sacred activity and become themselves the center of God's activity.

As radical as Luther's challenge in this sermon was in his own day, it is equally radical today within contemporary Lutheran understandings of both the sacrament and the theology of the cross. Whereas the majority of Luther scholarship has focused on what happens between God and the individual in the Lord's Supper, this sermon calls attention to Luther's communal understanding of God's activity. The sacramental debates with Zwingli and others do not exhaust Luther's understanding of the Lord's Supper as important as they might be. Luther never renounces the primary significance of the sacrament as community and continues to pick up this theme in sermons throughout his career that have unfortunately not been translated into English.[13]

If community is what distinguishes the gift that God gives to the faithful, then suffering or adversity characterizes the human condition in the absence of the divine gift. "Suffering [*Leide*] attacks us not only in one manner."[14] The term I translate here suffering also means pain, affliction, or even, when used in the plural, passion as in the passion of Christ. This word appears many times throughout the sermon. Luther identifies four ways that suffering assails Christians.[15] First, there is the sin that remains in us after baptism and that assails us as long as we live. Second, evil spirits unceasingly assail us with sins and afflictions. Third, the world that is full of wickedness irritates and persecutes us. It has no good on any side. Finally, our own guilty conscience assails us with the memory of past sins inspiring fear of both death and the pain of hell. Sin is not conceived simply or even principally as something that one does, but rather has the character of a force that enslaves

13. See, for example, WA 12(2).486.1; WA 45.525.29; WA TR 3, No. 3868; WA 46.98.7; WA 28.184.13.

14. Trans. mine, LW 35.53; WA 2.744.19.

15. LW 35.53; WA 2.744–45.

and attacks. The consistent grammatical positioning of humans in the above listed ways of assault is the accusative place, not the nominative, of the first person plural. Sin seems to be less an action or possession of ours than that which possesses and attacks us. Even in the first and the fourth examples wherein sin does its damage from within us through its remainder with us or through our guilty conscience, this sin attacks *our own selves.* Also Luther seems uninterested in clear distinctions between the suffering others cause us and the suffering that our own sin causes in us.

Ultimately his concern is for the fruit of consolation and the strength to struggle against sin in all its forms. Christ is the one who will bring us these benefits, not so much by assailing the assailant, but by allowing himself to be assailed by the same perpetrators.

Christ, usually together with all the saints, takes on human cares and sufferings making them his own. He is the initiator of the new reality in light of his own self-giving. Luther has Christ saying to the community of faith:

> I shall be the first to give myself for you all. I will make your sufferings and misfortune common to me and bear them for you all. As a result of this and in response, you all also may do likewise for me and mutually for one another, even allowing all things to be held in common in me and with me.[16]

Human sufferings become Christ's; human sufferings are yet another passion that Christ endures with the suffering people:

> Therefore, in this sacrament a sure sign from God Godself is given . . . that one is thus united with Christ and his saints and that all things are held in common, that their sufferings [or "passion"] and life are one's own, and they are also the shared life and sufferings of all the saints. Therefore whoever causes suffering for that one, causes it for Christ and all the saints.[17]

The theme of community builds upon themes already presented in the *Heidelberg Disputation.* Sufferings or crosses are the place where Christ is present and his love manifest. Together with the assurance that Christ is the suffering companion is the promise that Christ's strength is also given in the struggle against that which assails:

16. Trans. mine, cf. LW 35.55; WA 2.745.39.
17. Trans. mine, cf. LW 35.52; WA 2.744.8.

> Christ with all the saints through his love takes on our form, struggles with us against sin, death and all evil. Thereby a love is ignited in us to take on his form, to trust ourselves to his justice, life and blessedness, and thus to become one loaf, one bread, one body, one drink and have all things in common through the community of his goodness and our misfortune.[18]

Or again:

> be certain that Christ and all his saints are coming to you with all their virtues, sufferings, and mercies, to live, work, suffer and die with you, and that they desire to be wholly yours, having all things in common with you.[19]

If one combined the elements that Luther has identified as constitutive of community, one might gather together the images of shared suffering, mutual bearing of affliction, common struggle and communal goods. The word "solidarity" might be the most adequate single word to summarize all Luther wishes to say thus far about the gift of the sacrament. Yet, while turning to this word, it should not be forgotten that his concern is not only solidarity in suffering, but solidarity in our sinful condition. Part of that which we share in common is our sin or injustice. Thus even an emphasis on forgiveness has a communal significance. I take on your sins as my own, and you do the same for me, even as Christ has also done this for us. Together our voices rise to God, asking for forgiveness of the sins of us all. Therefore, the term solidarity in this community includes the responsibility among the faithful to "put up with sinners."[20]

Luther's understanding of the solidarity of Christ with us also includes the solidarity in our condition as sinners. In the case of those sins that remain within us after baptism, Christ does not place himself only between us and that which assails us (our sins, the devil, and the world), but also puts himself between God and us so that God's judgment might not be held against us. He is the one who intercedes in order to strengthen and encourage us. In the sacrament God sends Christ to us

18. Trans. mine, cf. LW 35.58; WA 2.748.14.

19. Trans mine, cf. LW 35.61; WA 2.750.8–10.

20. LW 35.57; WA 2.747.30.

for that very purpose to the effect that we might not waver, but might take heart and be courageous.[21]

This gift becomes operative through faith inspired by the sacrament, the preaching of the word and the mutual consolation of the faithful. The move from solitary suffering to believing in solidarity amidst suffering occurs through an act of faith. This faith comes through the proclaimed word of promise. Luther states that the near perishing of the communal understanding of the sacrament can be attributed to poor preaching.[22] He has Christ call on all the faithful to be preachers saying, "daily call to mind and admonish one another by means of what I did and am still doing for you all, in order that you all may be strengthened and also bear one another in the same way."[23]

This gift then is one of God's own giving. The sacrament is meant to have its effect upon us. Luther expects the sacrament to transform or transubstantiate us. It should stir and excite us beyond our most profound hopes and desires.[24] The fruit of the sacrament will be community, love and unity. Our first task is to give thanks for the gift and hold firmly to it.[25] And, then, as has already been indicated several times, to participate in God's solidarity by recognizing it and moving with it out toward others; we too take on the sufferings of the whole community since Christ has graciously taken on ours. Luther emphasizes that Christians cannot receive Christ's offer, while turning their back on the neighbor. One cannot have the benefits or profits (*geneissen*) of being a member of the community of solidarity, without also being willing to share the costs (*gelten*). Note the economic terms. Luther continually asserts that the only requirement for participation in this gift is desire, that we recognize our need, that we take hold of God's gifts.[26] But

> this sacrament is of little or no benefit to those who have no misfortune or anxiety, or who do not sense their adversity. For it is given only to those who need strength and comfort, who have timid hearts and terrified consciences, and who are assailed by

21. LW 35.53; WA 2.744.19–30.

22. LW 35.56; WA 2.747.7–10.

23. LW 35.55; WA 2.746.3–5.

24. LW 35.61; WA 2.750.20.

25. LW 35.65; WA 2.752.33.

26. See examples, LW 35.59; WA 2.749.6 and LW 35.65; WA 2.752.22.

sin, or have even fallen into sin. How could it do anything for
untroubled and secure spirits, who neither need nor desire it?[27]

This sacrament has no need for full or satisfied souls, but requires "a
sorrowing, hungry soul, who desires heartily the love, help and support of the entire community."[28] Luther claims that those who would
have Christ without the rest of the community receive death in the
sacrament.[29] Several themes from the *Heidelberg Disputation* are again
echoed here and made more concrete. He stresses the theme that seeking after goods or profits (*bonum/geneissen*) for one's own benefit at the
expense of others is sin. He also again warns of the dangers of seeking
one's own good or enjoyment while ignoring the neighbor in need.

Finally we come to the character of the community of solidarity
that is formed. One of the most lovely German words in the entire sermon describes the nature of the community as *fureinander*, that is to
say, the members of the community live for-one-another just as Christ
has so lived for them.[30] The community is especially concerned with
"the least"[31] or those who suffer most. This is contrasted well in a later
part of the essay. Luther criticizes those who

> like to hear that in this sacrament the help, community, and sup-
> port of all the saints are promised and given to them. But they
> are unwilling in their turn to belong also to this community.
> They will not help the poor, put up with sinners, care for the
> sorrowing, suffer with the suffering, intercede for others, defend
> the truth, and at the risk of life, property and honor seek the
> betterment of the church and of all Christians.[32]

He states, "They are self-serving (*eigenutzige*) people, for whom the
sacrament does no service (*Nutz*)."[33] Mutuality and solidarity charac-
terize the community. Through these practices the faith that receives
the gift is strengthened. The members are to put their sufferings before
the community and even place those sufferings on the community

27. LW 35.55; WA 2.746.17–20.

28. LW 35.65; WA 2.752.18–22.

29. LW 35.62; WA 2.750.35.

30. LW 35.52; WA 2.743.40.

31. LW 35.52; WA 2.744.15.

32. Trans. altered, LW 35–57; WA 2.747.25.

33. Trans. mine, cf. LW 35.57; WA 2.747.36.

and especially upon Christ.[34] They are to listen to the sufferings of the community and bear them together with Christ. Thus the sacrament contains both gift and challenge.

> There your heart must go out in love and learn that this is a sacrament of love. Just as love and support are given you, you in turn must give love and support to Christ through his needy ones. You must feel with sorrow all the dishonor done to Christ in his holy Word, all the misery of Christendom, all the unjust sufferings of the innocent, with which the whole world is everywhere filled to overflowing. You must fight, work, pray, and—if you cannot do more—have heartfelt compassion.[35]

Having laid out the nature of the true community, Luther then turns to critique what he sees as a mockery of that true body: the confraternities. His criticisms of these fraternal organizations are that their chief fruits are gluttony and drunkenness. They desecrate the names of the saints whom they supposedly seek to honor. In fact they are so disgraceful that "if a sow were made the patron saint of such a brotherhood she would not consent."[36] In addition, the goals of these groups are self-serving. They are a "simulated brotherhood."[37] Luther states that the true community of faith is based on "one baptism, one Christ, one sacrament, one food, one Gospel, one faith, one Spirit, one spiritual body."[38] He contrasts this with the confraternities whose unity is based on "one roll, one mass, one kind of good works, one festival day, one fee; and, as things are now, their common beer, common gluttony, and common drunkenness."[39] He finally calls upon them to reshape their community in light of the true sacramental community of Christ and all his saints; they should be servants of the world united in Christ alone.

Several themes of the theology of the cross in the *Heidelberg Disputation* have been carried forward in this sermon. Faith, in particular, continues to be emphasized. Faith sees a new reality and clings to it. Luther also again speaks of those who look towards what serves them, but who seem incapable of seeing the poor around them. Also some

34. LW 35.53; WA 2.745.4, 9.
35. Trans. altered, LW 35.54; WA 2.745.24.
36. LW 35.68; WA 2.754.36.
37. LW 35.69; WA 2.755.18.
38. LW 35.70; WA 2.756.23–25.
39. LW 35.71; WA 2.756.27–29.

themes that were implicit in the earlier disputation are made much more clear. The connection between Christ's cross on Golgotha and the crosses experienced by those who suffer in daily life is rigorously commended to the reader. The basis of this connection is the divine act of solidarity wherein Christ comes through the supper and once again takes on the suffering of the people. This solidarity is so profound that the community of faith is truly transformed into the body of Christ in history. Eucharistic language of transubstantiation and real presence are used by Luther to speak of the radical change that Christ effects. Because of this commitment of Christ, Luther claims that suffering that anyone inflicts upon another, they inflict upon Christ himself. The solidarity of Christ is contagious to believers. Through the gift of Christ they are brought into solidarity with one another. They are to turn toward those who are in need, who suffer dishonor, or who are innocent and suffer unjustly. Missing in this sermon is an explicit critique of generic human sinfulness so prevalent in the *Heidelberg Disputation*. Rather, in this proclamation, specific sin is named: the ignoring of those who suffer, seeking self-satisfaction while ignoring the needs of the "least," pursuing drunkenness and gluttony while forgetting the hurting neighbor in whom Christ is present. This move to the concrete repeats what I claimed was implicit in the *Heidelberg Disputation* until it became explicit at the end of his argument. In the earlier debate, Luther's generic critique of humanity functioned strategically as a concrete criticism of scholastic and ecclesiastic pretensions to power, prestige and profits. Here that criticism is even more clear.

Commentary on the *Magnificat*

In 1520 and 1521, Luther created one of his most beautiful devotional tracts, his *Commentary on the Magnificat*. As the storms of controversy were growing, Luther reflected on the poor woman whom God chose to bear the Christ. Luther wrote this piece as a teacher of the Bible, but also as the pastor of the people at Wittenberg. The fiasco of the Diet at Worms exploded in the middle of the writing and publication of this commentary; the later, finished text is clearly marked by this violent event.

On March 31, 1521, two days before Luther was to begin his trip to Worms, he sent a published portion of the commentary to the Prince

John Frederick. In the letter that Luther sent with it, he commented that one quire was still at the printers and more commentary was yet to be written.[40] Luther was not to finish his manuscript until June 10, 1521. The interruption in writing coupled with the completed printing of the early portion opens up an interesting window into the shifts within the Reformation movement. This single work contains Luther's biblical reflections immediately before the trial at Worms and then his continued reflections on the same scripture immediately after the Diet. A shift in Luther's hermeneutic is quite evident. Thus, besides its intrinsic worth as a commentary on Mary's song, this document offers an unintentional commentary on the change of focus that Luther underwent as a result of his experiences in Worms. The text records and exemplifies the moment of transition when Luther's Reformation moves in new directions.

The Explosion

In the summer of 1520, Rome had declared Luther a heretic. This serious charge could lead to execution by the state. In an unexpected turn of events, Luther was summoned to appear before the imperial authorities at the Diet of Worms during the month of April of 1521. The "invitation" that the emperor Charles V sent to Luther claimed that he desired Luther's presence in order to "obtain information from you about your doctrines and books . . ."[41] He guaranteed Luther safe conduct to and from the Diet. When Luther appeared before the imperial court, he was ambushed. Charles did not request a clarification of Luther's doctrines, but a recantation of his whole corpus. The Diet demanded an unadorned yes or no to the following questions: Do you, Martin Luther, recognize the books published under your name as your own? Are you prepared to recant what you have written in these books?

Once the names of the books had been read, Luther affirmed his authorship of them. In regards to the second question he requested additional time to prepare his response. He was reluctantly granted another day. When he appeared before the court this time his response was clear. He explained that the nature of the materials in question was diverse and thus could not possibly be recanted as a corpus. Some

40. Introduction to vol. 21, viii. The part which was finished and sent to the printers pre–Worms corresponds to what precedes, "True humility . . ." on LW 21.315.

41. Oberman, *Luther*, 35.

merely taught what the church always has taught and thus should not be recanted even according to his opponents. Others were opposed to papal tyranny that destroys the gospel; these could not be recanted without complicity with the tyrants. And then finally others were polemic in nature and, though harsh in tone, were still embraced until otherwise refuted. The now famously audacious response then followed:

> Unless I am convinced by the testimony of the Holy Scriptures or by evident reason—for I can believe neither pope nor councils alone, as it is clear that they have erred repeatedly and contradicted themselves—I consider myself convicted by the testimony of Holy Scripture, which is my basis; my conscience is captive to the Word of God. Thus I cannot and will not recant, because acting against one's conscience is neither safe nor sound. God help me. Amen.[42]

Luther suffered a trial that had nothing to do with the quest for truth. Luther desired to debate the merits of his perspective on the basis of scripture, but he was not allowed even to expound these. Neither did his opponents refute those beliefs on the basis of scripture. The emperor acted as little more than a hired hand of Rome and showed no interest in hearing Luther out.

The Text before Worms

In the portion of the text written before the Diet, what did Luther see in the *Magnificat*? For Luther, Mary's identity and her selection by God are the concrete realities through which one understands the song that she raises. Mary praises God's act on behalf of people like herself and against those who are in conflict with her people. Who then is Mary?

Luther does not abandon traditional language for Mary. In the opening phrase of the treatise, he calls her the Blessed Virgin Mary and later the Mother of God. Yet we should not be led too far astray by his use of traditional language. What is finally important about Mary is her particular social location or "her low estate." Luther specifies exactly whom God has chosen in Mary:

> Let us make it very plain for the sake of the simple. Doubtless there were in Jerusalem daughters of the chief priests and counselors who were rich, comely, youthful, cultured, and

42. Ibid., 39.

held in high renown by all the people; even as it is today with
the daughters of kings, princes, and men of wealth. The same
was also true of many another city. Even in her own town of
Nazareth she was not the daughter of one of the chief rulers, but
a poor and plain citizen's daughter, whom none looked up to
or esteemed. To her neighbors and their daughters she was but
a simple maiden, tending cattle and doing the housework, and
doubtless esteemed no more than any poor maidservant today,
who does as she is told around the house.[43]

For the sake of the simple folk, a designator for those who have
not received formal education, Luther proclaims that Mary was a
"simple maiden." Luther places this same focus on social location in
the mouth of Mary herself, "God has regarded me, a poor, despised, and
lowly maiden, though He might have found a rich, renowned, noble,
and mighty queen, the daughter of princes and great lords."[44] Mary's
social location renders her nothing in the eyes of her world; and the
same could be said of "any poor maidservant today." Society's negative
view of Mary is made relentlessly clear as nasty words are piled high
upon her.

The divine choosing of poor Mary reveals the very nature of God.
Her election is the paradigm of God's activity. As in the *Heidelberg
Disputation*, the first chapter of 1 Corinthians is again invoked by Luther,
"God chose what is foolish in the world to shame the wise. God chose
what is low and despised in the world, even things that are not, to bring
to nothing things that are."[45] Luther wants to make clear that "what is
foolish" or "low and despised" refers to the poor in their specific social
location and not to the rich. He repeatedly refuses to accept that this is
a reference to a personal disposition or attitude of humility that Mary
possesses. When all of scripture including this hymn speaks of humility,
it refers to "nothing else than a disregarded, despised, and lowly estate,
such as that of those who are poor, sick, hungry, thirsty, in prison, suffering and dying."[46] And again he insists that those "of low degree are
here not the humble, but all those who are contemptible and altogether

43. LW 21.301; WA 7.548.34–549.7.

44. LW 21.314; WA 7.560.36–561.2.

45. 1 Corinthians 1:28, 29, as quoted by Luther at LW 21.313–14; WA 7.560.28–34.

46. Trans. altered, LW 21.313; WA 7.560.16–19. Also see LW 21.317; WA 7.563.29.

nothing in the eyes of the world."[47] In the *Heidelberg Disputation* the theme that the poor are nothing in the eyes of the powerful was raised in the final thesis. Luther had written, "For this reason, [in the eyes the theologian of glory] the object of comprehension cannot be that which is nothing, that is, the poor or destitute. . . ."[48] This theme that was laid bare at the end of the *Heidelberg Disputation* takes center stage throughout this early commentary on the poor Mary's song as it did in the sermon we just studied.

The *Heidelberg Disputation* focused on the tension between human pretensions or powers and God's gracious gift. Luther had stressed the tension between self-justification by law or labor and God's free justification. The tension throughout the *Commentary on the Magnificat* takes on a different issue. Luther's focus now has shifted to the conflict between the kind of person that the world consistently chooses (the rich, the honored, the powerful) and the kind whom God always chooses (the poor, the dishonored ones, the marginalized). Luther lays bare the contrast between the way that the world treats Mary and the way that God does. This tension finds itself embedded in the language of the text itself. The translator often is forced to make a choice between translating from the world's perspective or from God's. For example, early in its translation *Luther's Works* offers the following rendering:

> When the holy virgin experienced what great things God was working in her *despite* her insignificance, lowliness, poverty, and inferiority, the Holy Spirit taught her this deep insight and wisdom. . . .[49]

This is a grammatically permissible translation, yet I would translate it:

> When the holy virgin experienced what great things God was working in her—*yes, her!* insignificant, lowly, poor, and inferior—the Holy Spirit taught her this deep insight and wisdom.[50]

The German word upon which the different translations hinge is *doch. Luther's Work* sees this indicating contradiction, "despite." Yet it is better translated as creating an emphatic assertion. According to the full

---

47. LW 21.345; WA 7.591.11.

48. Trans. mine, cf. LW 31.57–58; WA 1.365.17–18.

49. LW 21.299 (emphasis mine); WA 7.546.30–31.

50. Trans. mine, cf. LW 21.299; WA 7.546.30–31.

treatise, God does not act despite Mary's poverty, but because of it. The use of "despite" suggests that another human medium would have been more appropriate, perhaps a rich woman or a queen. This, of course, is the world's appraisal; God's appraisal of the situation is that there is no more appropriate station for divine work. This tension is continually present in the text. Many of the adjectives applied to Mary and others like her would be faithfully rendered in quotation marks to suggest that, for example, Mary is only "inferior" in the eyes of the world, not in the eyes of God.

Luther broke with much of the Mariology that had proceeded. Luther vehemently attacked those who seek virtue in Mary as the grounds for God's election:

> But the masters who so depict and portray the blessed Virgin that there is found in her nothing to be despised, but only great and lofty things—what are they doing but contrasting us with her instead of her with God?[51]

They are "fulsome eulogists and empty chatterers" who claim for Mary what she denied for herself. They are calling her a liar since she wishes to claim nothing of her own merit and gives all the glory to God. "Mary also freely ascribes all to God's grace, not to her merit . . . Though certain scribblers make much ado about her worthiness for such motherhood, I prefer to believe her rather than them."[52] Mary sings this song not to glorify herself, but to draw us into the salvation of God. "She does not want you to come to her, but through her to God."[53] It is then appropriate to follow Luther's advice and the direction of Mary's song, and turn toward the one of whom she sings.

According to Luther, God is the central theme of Mary's song. This song teaches three things: the proper fear of God in faith, God's character, and God's dealing with both the low and the high.[54] In the first paragraph of commentary on the text, Luther clearly sets the tone for the whole piece. He challenges his readers to shift their perspective from human disregard to God's regarding of who is high and who is lowly. Through the grammatical shape of his commentary Luther works

51. LW 21.323; WA 7.569.12–15.
52. LW 21.327; WA 7.573.4–8.
53. LW 21.323; WA 7.560.8–9.
54. LW 21.298; WA 7.545.20–22.

out in writing his view on what kind of God is working in history. God is revealed as

> the kind of Lord who accomplishes nothing else than only exalting [*erhohen*] those who are lowly [*was ist niedrig*], and lowering [*niedern*] those who are exalted [*was da hoch ist*], in short, who breaks [*brechen*] what is established [*ist gemacht*] and who establishes [*machen*] what is broken [*brochen ist*].[55]

Notice the X Y Y' X' pattern that gives shape to his reading: *erhohen/ist* nied*rig*/nied*ern/ist* hoch and brech*en/ist* ge*macht/machen/* broch*en ist*. This is not at all clear grammatically in the rendering by *Luther's Works*, "exalt those of low degree and put down the mighty from their thrones." In its translation of the second phrase the pattern is maintained, but the word choice misses the mark: "break what is whole and make whole what is broken."[56] Since Luther is pursuing a political metaphor as that translation accurately recognizes by inserting "thrones" into his text on the first phrase, then the issue is not wholeness, but establishment. Luther emphatically claims that this is the only way that God works. He combines the "nothing else" with "only" to create a categorical confession that this is the one and only way that one can count on God to work. Again, God chose and uplifted the Virgin Mary, not finally because of who she is in and of herself, but because of the kind of Lord that God is, that is, the God who always chooses the poor. This theme remains constant throughout the early commentary; of course, Luther is consistent with the biblical text itself. Verses 51 through 53 of Mary's song state:

> 51 He works wonders with his arm
> and scatters all who are arrogant
> in their own heart's opinion.
>
> 52 He unseats the great lords from their lordship,
> and he raises up there those who are lowly and nothing.
>
> 53 He makes the hungry satisfied with all good things.
> And the rich he allows to remain empty.[57]

---

55. Trans. mine, LW 21.299; WA 7.546.32–34.
56. LW 21.299; WA 7.546.32–34.
57. Trans. mine, WA 7.546.

Does this divine, preferential faithfulness to the poor compromise the gospel as radical gift? Is Mary's poverty now a kind of virtue that earns her God's grace? Luther would respond to both questions with a loud, "No!" Rather, the radical otherness of God and God's grace is shown in the fact that God always elects those whom the world neglects. Here otherness is not limited to ontological distinction, but carries theological and ethical weight. While the claim that this is the only way God will act may seem to limit God's freedom, it is a self-imposed limitation that comes from God's commitment to being the God of the poor. This affirmation can never be tame to the world; God's preference for the poor over the rich and powerful presents a perpetual scandal to the world.

Luther comments on the above text asking, "How can one know God better than in the works in which He is most Himself?" Luther goes on, "Whoever understands His works correctly cannot fail to know His nature and will, His heart and mind."[58] Just as Mary is the paradigm for the person that God always chooses, so the works mentioned in these verses are paradigmatic of the way that God acts. When performing them, God is most godly, that is, God is most consonant with God's own character.

This kind of action on God's part is nothing new; God has acted in this way from the beginning. Early in the essay, Luther invokes the understanding of creation out of nothing. He does this to ground his understanding of what might be called re-creation out of nothing. He writes:

> Just as God in the beginning of creation made the world out of nothing, whence He is called the Creator and the Almighty, so His manner of working continues unchanged. Even now and to the end of the world, all His works are such that out of that which is nothing, worthless, despised, wretched, and dead, He makes that which is something, precious, honorable, blessed and living.[59]

Notice that in the translation above Luther has inserted the word "nothing" into verse 52 though it does not exist in the Greek. He builds upon this theme then in the above quotation.

58. LW 21.331; WA 7.546.10–15.
59. LW 21.299; WA 7.547.1–5.

In this pre-Diet part of his essay, Luther associates "nothing" with a social estate in which people like Mary live. The commentary then continues, "On the other hand, whatever is something, precious, honorable, blessed and living, He makes to be nothing, worthless, despised, wretched, and dying."[60] The consistency of God's actions is echoed in the balance and symmetry of Luther's commentary on the reversal mentioned in the biblical text. Each negative has a positive: nothing/something, worthless/precious, despised/honorable, wretched/blessed, dead/living. Also, both of the series of words are repeated unaltered in this parallel structure with the single, interesting exception of the shift from "is dead" to "be dying." In the midst of the consistency of God's action, Luther breaks with his established pattern. Though God might afflict the established, God apparently does not bring death itself to their house.

Obviously Luther does not only have Mary's social location in mind, but also another social location that he describes in many ways: established, rich, cultured, well-known, rulers, lords, exalted, arrogant, something, precious, honorable, blessed, living. These descriptors are diametrically opposed to the estate of Mary who is broken, poor, uncultured, unknown, a maid, a servant, lowly, nothing, worthless, despised, wretched, and encompassed by death. This leads Luther to claim that the world is deeply divided, and for this reason, God's word cuts in two distinct directions. Faith in the word "constrains you to fear if you are mighty, and to take comfort if you are of low degree. And the mightier you are, the more you must fear; the lowlier you are, the more you must take comfort."[61] The heart of this hymn of praise is "the great works and deeds of God, for the strengthening of our faith, for the comforting of all those of low degree, and for the terrifying of all the mighty ones of earth."[62] Mary sings of a divided world:

> Hence to understand His works is an art. And in order that we may learn it, Mary enumerates . . . six divine works among as many classes of people. She divides all the world into two parts either side has its exact counterpart in the other. She describes the works of God in each of these two parts, portraying Him so

60. LW 21.299; WA 7.547.5–7.
61. LW 21.306; WA 7.553.35–554.2.
62. LW 21.306; WA 7.563.17–20.

well that it could not be done better. This division is well conceived and is borne out by other passages of scripture.[63]

Luther goes on to state that the classes are constituted by the three categories of the wise, the mighty, and the rich over and against the poor in
spirit, the oppressed, and those who lack the necessities of life.[64]

Two words need to be mentioned at this point. First of all, Luther's
proclamation of the gospel directs itself in a special way to his context;
he proclaims "for the sake of the simple." Luther has not only chosen to
understand Mary as a poor woman, but also has cast her in a particular
vocation; she is a domestic servant in Luther's rendering. Remember
that Germany was structured hierarchically based upon different estates. Luther has focused on Mary in terms of this structuring and how
her assigned estate made her nothing in the eyes of the powerful. When
imagining the estate of Mary, Luther went down to the bottom of the
pyramidal structure of his world to the low status of the domestic servant. What is more, he chose that specific vocation with which a large
percentage of his public could identify on the basis of firsthand experience. As stated earlier, a large portion of the urban population, including a disproportionate number of those who migrated from rural areas,
lived as domestic servants for as long as two decades of their life. They
constituted a large portion of the urban have-nots. Luther has brought
together the social ranking of Mary who is practically nothing in the
eyes of the world with the theological confession of God who creates
out of nothing.

The strategy of proclaiming the gospel in the pre-Worms segment
of the commentary appears in Luther's choice of a social location for
Mary. She is described in such a way that those at the bottom of the
social structure understand her situation as their own. Luther proclaims
through the concrete metaphor of the poor domestic Mary how God
is for the poor who might hear the word of this commentary. Luther
has chosen a numerically common vocation in order to drive home the
message to the vast majority of the poor that God has chosen them as
God chose Mary. How striking it must have been for the poor to see the
Queen of Heaven reimagined in their own image!

63. LW 21.331; WA 7.577.28–35.

64. LW 21.332; WA 7.578.5–8.

In this commentary Luther maps out the entrenched divisions in his world; in the *Heidelberg Disputation*, at a first glance in any case, Luther demonstrates little concern for recognizing such rifts in his world. All humanity within earshot is condemned. Yet those within earshot at that disputation conducted in Latin were universally from the educated and powerful strata of his world. Even those who had not gained status through their parentage had inherited it through their role in wealthy Mother Church. Especially compared to a poor domestic, they had access to privilege, power, and prestige. The *Heidelberg Disputation*'s devastating critique of human pretension was so rigorous because, given the audience, the word's work was to break down those who were established rather than to establish those who are broken. This commentary continued this divine work, but also reached to the very bottom to comfort and transform the poor.

After Worms

In the pre-Worms segment of his commentary, Luther had focused upon God's election of Mary in light of her social location as an oppressed person. This was contrasted with those not so chosen, the mighty and the rich. Yet in his commentary after Worms, Luther focuses much more on another pairing. Not the rich verses the poor, but the wise verses the "poor in spirit" take center stage. In the later installment of the commentary, Luther claims unabashedly that the greatest reprobates are not those who exploit the poor, but rather those who believe that they are wise. Luther argues, "No rich or mighty man is so puffed up and bold as one such smart aleck who feels and knows that he is in the right, understands all about a matter, and is wiser than other people."[65] He goes on to explore the actions of these most puffed up people. They "boast of being infallible." What is more, they violently oppose all who hold ideas contrary to their own. Luther writes:

> If such a man possesses the necessary power, he rushes on headlong, persecuting, condemning, slandering, slaying, banishing, and destroying all who differ with him, saying afterward he did it all to the honor and glory of God.[66]

65. LW 21.332–33; WA 7.578.33–579.1.
66. LW 21.333; WA 7.579.5–8.

Luther continues his complaint, "Such people will not give you a hearing; it is impossible that they should be in the wrong or give way."[67] Luther's vocabulary is telling: infallible, persecuting, condemning. Clearly this section had been based on his own experience at the Diet of Worms. In fact, he clarifies this rather quickly.

> Such, above all others, are the pope and his herd today and these many days. They do all of these things, and worse than were ever done; there is no hearing nor giving way, it profits nothing to speak, to counsel, beg or threaten. It is simply, "We are in the right," and there is an end of it, in spite of everyone else, though it be the whole world.[68]

A major shift definitively has taken place in Luther's interpretation of the biblical text. His own intense experience at the Diet of Worms shifted his interpretation. In the beginning of the essay, the poor woman Mary is the paradigm of the one whom God elects, and so the exalted ones who oppose her are interpreted primarily in terms of political power (thrones) and wealth. After Worms, Luther himself unseats Mary and takes her place as the paradigm of God's elect one. The poor Mary falls out of his focus. In the beginning of this commentary, her poverty and low estate are of the essence. In the end, Luther's experience of being attacked by the papacy preempts the biblical image of poor Mary.

Luther's focus on the election of the poor is lost as he tries to establish the righteousness of his own confession. Luther takes the focus off of God's promise to the poor and powerless, and shifts it to God's promise to Luther and others who are opposed by the Roman Church's authorities in their capacity as theologians. While we have seen in previous chapters that the poor and powerless felt opposed by the institutional church, the sharpness of the earlier sections where issues of economics and status were at the forefront has been blunted. Luther has come to believe that the tyranny that he himself experiences is the more violent and pressing concern. Mary and her people got lost in Luther's own struggles and the resulting hermeneutical shift. The concreteness of Luther's proclamation of God's graciousness "for you" to the poor is usurped in favor of Luther's own concrete experience. While the poor were still able to make the connection between themselves

---

67. LW 21.334; WA 7.580.7–12.
68. LW 21.334; WA 7.580.7–12.

and the silenced "Mary," the preaching has lost the specificity that is the stuff of good proclamation. Moreover, the biblical text itself suggests that the intuition of the early sections was more to the point. In the text of Mary's song, the "wise" are not mentioned specifically as are the rich and the lords, though Luther might argue that the "arrogant in their own heart's opinion" are those of whom he speaks.

Feeding the suspicion that some kind of betrayal of the poor is taking place is another new element. In the latter part of this commentary, Luther turns from God's reversal of social hierarchy toward the legitimizing of hierarchy. The *Magnificat* is not easily or faithfully pressed into such service! Luther now states, "There must needs be such [status] differences and distinctions among persons and stations in our life here on earth; yet the heart should neither cling to them nor fly from them."[69] Luther also now interprets humility in a spiritualized way, the very thing he outright condemned earlier. The wounded reformer asserts that distinctions between humans in the public sphere are necessary. God no longer only saves the poor. God saves those who do not cling to their riches with their hearts. The message has been softened if not outright corrupted through the translation of it into Luther's experience.

This text documents the major shift that took place as Luther's Reformation moved from speaking specifically to the plight of the poor toward the goal of establishing its own institutional security. This does not mean that at a particular date the reformer had nothing more to say to the poor. Luther continued to proclaim the gospel as he understood it. Much in his message was still refreshing to the poor. Yet, he turned from announcing the good news as a proclamation spoken specifically for the sake of the poor toward reframing that gospel in terms of the persecution of the Reformation movement itself in the struggle to establish its legitimacy. By establishing textually the legitimacy of his own "foolishness" in the eyes of God, Luther hoped to bring the powers that be to his side. This turn within the commentary from the specificity of the poor toward the struggle to establish Luther's own theological validity mirrors the change that the whole Reformation movement undergoes. The question that remains a living one today is whether the Reformation could have remained faithful both to the poor and to the rest of the enduring, lively evangelical traditions announced in

69. LW 21.346; WA 7.592.7–18.

the Reformation. Can the gospel as Luther understood it once again be concretely, specifically, and directly good news to the poor?

Some historians have argued that this shift was not a betrayal, but was a shift that was both necessary and appropriate. Steven Ozment states, "The reformers understood as profoundly as any that winning in history meant getting society's reigning institutions on one's side."[70] While not altogether unfounded as a historical argument, this understanding flies in the face of fundamental presuppositions of Luther's theology of the cross. God alone, not institutional support, will bring victory to God's true cause. To turn from Mary and her God in order to be occupied with the task of establishing even a righteous cause entails a break down in trusting the God who always and only chooses those who are nothing in the eyes of the world.

Yet, even though criticism of Luther's change of focus is in order, Luther has made an interesting move that has merit. Having laid out an understanding of how God works in relation to Mary, he makes the hermeneutical move of both interpreting his own experience of God's work in terms of Mary's experience and of reinterpreting—somewhat awkwardly but not all together inappropriately—Mary's song in light of his own experience. In both cases he deals with an imbalance in power relations mentioned in the text, but also that were present in Mary's context as well as his own. He moves Mary's confession from the mouth of a young peasant maiden at the beginning of the first century to his own mouth, that of a banned and condemned reformer of sixteenth-century Germany. This is not unrelated to what Luther sees as the intended function of Mary's hymn. The risk is that a less fatal and pervasive experience like that of Luther comes to overshadow the more general and deadly experience of massive poverty suffered by the majority of the simple folk.

Luther's experience is present implicitly in his later interpretation of this text, but what does Luther explicitly state about the role of experience in the confession of the faith? The opening lines of his commentary on the *Magnificat* make this very clear:

> In order properly to understand this sacred hymn of praise, we need to bear in mind that the Blessed Virgin Mary is speaking on the basis of her experience, in which she was enlightened

70. Ozment, *Protestants*, 23.

and instructed by the Holy Spirit. No one can correctly understand God or His Word unless he has received such understanding immediately from the Holy Spirit. But no one can receive it
from the Holy Spirit without experiencing, proving, and feeling
it. In such experience the Holy Spirit instructs us as in His own
school, outside of which nothing is learned but empty words
and prattle.[71]

Experience and feeling are given a fundamental role in shaping
Mary's confession. Also for all of the faithful, the kind of experience
that Mary enjoys is required for the integrity of their praise of God.
Luther even claims that this kind of praise "cannot be taught in words
but must be learned in one's own experience."[72] Yet Luther also offers
a very different appraisal of experience in this same commentary. Of
Mary's confession, he states, "Mary, therefore calls God her Savior, or
her Salvation, even though she neither saw nor felt that this was so, but
trusted in sure confidence that He was her Savior and her Salvation."[73]
A tension remains in Luther that God's grace is both experienced and
potentially not experienced, both felt and not felt, both revealed and
hidden. Above all, one must affirm that for Luther God's grace in the
strictest sense is not a part of Mary's ordinary, human experience.

What was the typically human experience of Mary? Mary's experience in her society would tell her that she is despised, nothing, worthless. Such experience, which Luther holds is the pervasive and sole
experience that she receives in the world, will not reveal anything about
divine graciousness. Her experience is that of being looked down upon
or of being completely ignored.

This we experience every day. Everyone strives after that which
is above him, after honor, power, wealth, knowledge, a life of
ease and whatever is lofty and great. And where such people are,
there are many hangers-on; all the world gathers round them,
gladly yields them service, and would be at their side and share
in their exaltation. Therefore it is not without reason that the
Scriptures describe so few kings and rulers who were godly men.
On the other hand, no one is willing to look into the depths with
their poverty, disgrace, squalor, misery, and anguish. From these
all turn away their eyes. Where there are such people, every-

71. LW 21.299; WA 7.546.21–29.
72. LW 21.302; WA 7.550.10–11.
73. LW 21.309; WA 7.556.13–16.

one takes to his heels, forsakes and shuns and leaves them to themselves.[74]

This theme was, of course, also in the *Heidelberg Disputation*, though it was not fully explored. Luther develops this theme of where humans "look" extensively in the commentary on Mary's song. Here though he is not speaking so much to those who look away as to those who are ignored, something that could not be said of the *Heidelberg Disputation*. He is pessimistic that humans will ever act any differently than this:

> For truth and right must always be assailed by the wise, the mighty and the rich, that is, by the world with its greatest and best ability. . . . The learned, saintly, mighty, great, and rich, and the best that the world has must fight against God and the right, and be the devil's own.[75]

Having explained the kind of perspective that humans employ, Luther contrasts it with God's way:

> Therefore to God alone belongs the sort of seeing that looks into the depths with their need and misery, and is near to all that are in the depths. . . . He is a God who looks into the depths and helps only the poor, despised, afflicted, miserable, forsaken and those who are nothing, there a hearty love for him is born.[76]

Thus with a striking double image Luther claims that God alone looks to the poor and also that God looks to the poor alone. This image of "divine looking" runs throughout the commentary, granting an amazingly transformative power to the gaze of divine compassion. The word for the "look" or gracious "regard" of God in German is *ansehen*. It first appears in Luther's translation of Mary's song itself:

46 My soul uplifts God, the Lord,

47 And my spirit rejoices in God, my Savior.

48 Because he *has regard* for me,
  his lowly servant;[77]

---

74. LW 21.300; WA 7.547.19–27.

75. LW 21.344; WA 7.590.23–25.

76. LW 21.300; WA 7.547.33–548.8.

77. Trans. mine, WA 7.546.2–5.

Within the commentary itself God's "look" interacts with other vocabulary to create an interesting play of words. Take this typical quotation:

> Now, we have said enough above as to the disregarded [*unan-sehlichs*] being and station of the tender Virgin and as to how unforeseeably [*unvorsehens*] this honor came that God has regarded [*hat angesehen*] her with such abundant grace. Therefore she does not praise her own worthiness nor even her own un-worthiness, but rather only God's regard [*Ansehens*] alone which is so exceedingly good and abundantly gracious that he even has regarded [*hat ansehenn*] such a poor girl and desires to regard [*ansehen*] her so gloriously and honorably.[78]

Depending how *unansehlichs* and *ansehen* are rendered, some of the possible translations might be: God regards the disregarded one, sees the unsightly one, looks to the poor-looking one, favors the ill-favored one or respects the disrespected! This divine respect or regard is transformative. Again Luther stresses:

> Mary confesses that the foremost work God did for her was that He regarded her, which is indeed the greatest of His works, on which all the rest depend and from which they all derive. For where it comes to pass that God turns His face [*Angesicht*] to-ward one to regard him, there is nothing but grace and salva-tion, and all gifts and works must follow.[79]

This reversal caused by the divine gaze becomes the basis upon which Mary experiences, proves, and feels the newness of the word. An experience diametrically opposed to her common experience comes to her. The alternative offered in the divine verdict over Mary challenges and overcomes her daily, dehumanizing experience. Mary's bondage is not a generic enslavement of the will, but the experience of being trapped by a society that despises her. The Spirit fills and transforms Mary through a liberation from her own particular enslavement. Luther imagines Mary saying,

> My life and all of my senses are suspended in God's love, praise and lofty joy. Thus I, not by my own strength, become more exalted toward God's praise than I might be exalted by myself.

78. Trans. mine, LW 21.314; WA 7.561.8–13.
79. LW 21.321; WA 7.567.24–28.

> Thus it happens to all those who become an overflowing chan-
> nel of God's sweetness and Spirit that they feel more than they
> can say.[80]

The Holy Spirit brings Mary to awareness of God's act and raises this song within her. The Spirit flows through her and every like believer suspending them in a radically alternative reality in which the grace of God rules. In the giving of God's promise, Mary experiences the whole world made new. Mary "is caught up, as it were, into [God] and feels herself lifted up into His good and gracious will."[81] Luther waxes poetic in describing the fruit of the experience of God's regard, "The heart overflows with gladness and goes leaping and dancing for the great pleasure it has found in God."[82] God's ever-so-different, gracious ruling has snatched Mary from the world's enslavement of her. This kind of experience of grace generates faith; this is not our own doing, but is "the work of God in us."[83] This divine work called faith is the mode by which God works with God's people.[84] They have, again by God's act, "a firm confidence in the unseen grace of God."[85]

Luther's tension between whether or not God's gift is felt and expe-rienced begins to make sense. Certainly Luther wishes to deny any pos-sibility of this being felt on the basis of Mary's own social experience. Yet when God acts, she does experience the alternative reality through the promise received in faith. Though all the world look down upon Mary and all the poor people, those who are poor know through God's active love and regard for them that they are God's beloved chosen ones. This reality defies the world's way of seeing things but is nonetheless real. The grace of God is hidden in Mary. Luther writes:

> What great things are hidden under this lowly exterior! How
> many came in contact with her, talked and ate and drank with
> her, who perhaps despised her and counted her but a common,
> poor, and simple village maiden.[86]

80. Trans. mine, cf. LW 21.302; WA 7.550.5–8.

81. LW 21.307; WA 7.554.21–22.

82. LW 21.300; WA 7.548.8–10.

83. LW 21.303; WA 7.550.17.

84. LW 21.318; WA 7.565.19–20.

85. LW 21.305; WA 7.552.22–23.

86. LW 21.329; WA 7.575.23–24.

The theme from the *Disputation* of hiddenness is presented here with an interesting twist. Just as the greatest gift of God was hidden in Jesus on the cross, so great divine things are hidden in the lowly domestic servant Mary. The cross and Mary's lowly social location are joined together in their role of bearing the divine presence in a way that the world refuses to see. The eyes of faith are able to see from God's perspective what is hidden to the world. The faithful "lay hold on things incomprehensible, invisible and eternal."[87] Through faith they comprehend and see the new reality precisely in their temporal existence. They receive the new reality of God. For the "believing spirit alone possesses all things."[88]

Mary learns not only God's general goodness, but of how God is good to her in particular. Luther has already sown the seeds for this particular dynamic in the translation of the original biblical text that he has provided:

46 My soul uplifts *God*, the Lord,

47 And my spirit rejoices in God, my Savior.

48 Because he has looked to *me*,
his lowly servant;
Therefore the children's children
will eternally exalt me.

49 Because he, *who created [thuet] all things,*
has created [*hat gethan*] great things for me
and holy is his name.

The above italics indicate the phrases that Luther adds to the original scriptural text as a kind of embedded gloss. In the first verse, Luther inserts the word "God" into the text before "the Lord." This sets up a parallel structure between verses 46 and 47. First of all, there is the recognition that God is God or Lord. But then one can almost hear Luther whisper to Mary, "What does this mean?" To which she responds, "I believe that God, the true God, the Lord . . . is *my* Savior." By the simple addition of the word God into the first phrase, Luther hints at the pattern that will later dictate his work on the creed in the *Small Catechism*. "God is good in Godself, but, more to the point, God is thus *for me*," Mary can confess. In the very next phrase Luther again inserts "to me," in order to rein-

87. LW 21.303; WA 7.550.29–30.
88. LW 21.305; WA 7.552.30–31.

force this same dynamic. The longest insertion that Luther incorporates into the text is found in verse 49; he adds the phrase, "who created all things" (*der alle ding thuet*) which prefaces Mary's own assertion: "has created great things for me" (*hat grosz ding mir gethan*). Again the move is from God acting universally to the God whom Mary can concretely declare acts for her sake. Luther uses the grammatical sharing of the same subject by the two clauses with the repetition of the same verb and direct object in the clauses to stress his point.

The fountain from which Mary's experience springs forth is the realization that God acts particularly on her behalf. To know that God is the Lord without knowing that God is her Savior is inadequate knowledge, for ". . . every one of us should pay attention to what God does for him rather than to all the works He does for others."[89] Yet Luther is not finished with this assertion. Though it is through this experience of God's act on one's behalf that faith bubbles up, faith ultimately seeks to lead even away from the gifts that God gives to trust in God in God's "naked goodness."

Ultimately Mary does not cling to the gift of this intimate experience, but moves even beyond it to God alone. Luther claims that ". . . we must not fall upon the good gifts of God or boast of them, but make our way through them . . . to Him, cling to Him alone, and highly esteem His goodness."[90] Faith is most itself when it clings to the grace of God against the all-pervasive indications to the contrary, even when God's goodness is completely hidden. For this reason, Luther values that suffering which may even be viewed as coming from God's own hand; it has the potential of teaching us to cleave to God alone.

> The purpose of the many sufferings, of death, and all manner
> of afflictions we have to bear on earth; by means of trouble and
> pain they cause us, we are to pluck out the evil eye.[91]

Mary demonstrates pure faith by her heart that is the same in all circumstances.[92]

I find Luther least helpful here. My suspicions are aroused again in that the theme of the edifying nature of Mary's suffering comes in

89. LW 21.318; WA 7.565.2–5.

90. LW 21.318; WA 7.564.30–33.

91. LW 21.317; WA 7.564.3–5.

92. LW 21.309; WA 7.556.7–9.

the post-Worms reflections. This understanding of God's activity can easily degenerate into a justification not of the sinner, but of the sinful, unjust and ungodly circumstances that humans create for one another. Even here though, Luther's approach is not totally without redemption. It does serve several functions that I believe are laudable. First of all, Luther calls the poor to hope in God's goodness even when all else seeks to condemn them. If this can be reshaped into an active hope for struggle against unjust situations, this is indeed liberative. Secondly, Luther calls all to trust that God will be God and that hope must ultimately reside in God alone. Finally, Luther calls on the faithful to ever seek solidarity in a downward movement, against the human ascending tendency that Luther indicated so poignantly, toward those yet more lowly and oppressed. The model of Mary is as one who, though God richly blesses her, "does not think of any poor serving maid as beneath her."[93]

While not accepting totally Luther's portrayal of God as the cause of suffering, sufferers themselves often note how much stronger their faith became in situations of intense suffering. Outside of such suffering, for example, in the comfort of an opulent church, things are understood differently. Luther is very appropriate in recognizing that when this song is taken out of its stark context and moved into a new one filled with "gorgeous pomp" "the more often we sing it [in such a context], the more we silence its true music and meaning."[94]

Finally, however, the goal of the *Magnificat* is not only that we know what God did for Mary,

> but for us all, to sing it after her. . . . In fact, it is not even enough to believe He is willing to do them for others but not for you. This would be to put yourself beyond the pale of these works of God, as is done by those who, because of their strength, do not fear Him, and by those of little faith who, because of their tribulations, fall into despair.
>
> That sort of faith is nothing; it is dead; it is like an idea learned from a fairy tale. You must rather, without wavering or doubt, realize His will toward you and firmly believe that He will do great things also to you and is willing to do so. Such a faith has life and being; it pervades and changes the whole person; it constrains you to fear if you are mighty, and to take comfort if you are of low degree. And the mightier you are, the

93. LW 21.308; WA 7.555.35.
94. Ibid.

more must you fear; the lowlier you are, the more must you take comfort.[95]

While we are all to sing with Mary, we are not all automatically to assume that we are like Mary. While the lowly are to trust that God will raise them up, the rest of us singing Mary's song are awaiting something quite different for ourselves. To live faithfully according to Mary's song is to step down from our privileges in order to see Mary and her people around us with God's eyes. We would do well at this point to recall that Luther's essay was dedicated to Prince John Frederick. The ruler's decisions will affect Mary and her people:

> For the welfare of many people lies in the power of so mighty
> a prince, once he is taken out of himself and graciously governed by God; on the other hand, the destruction of many people lies in his power if he is left to himself and ruled by God's
> displeasure.[96]

The rich and powerful do not love this song because it threatens all that they hold dear. Yet when we cling to all that we hold dear, God, the particular kind of God that Mary confesses, cannot be dear to us and our cause is hopeless. If we reject Mary and solidarity with her, Luther sees our cause as lost, "For unless a lord and ruler loves his subjects and has for his chief concern not how to live at ease but how to uplift and improve his people, his case is hopeless."[97] On those rare occasions, where the high and mighty learn to sing and live rightly with Mary, there is true life, blessedness, and salvation.

In this commentary, Luther has deepened his theology of the cross in some of the directions already hinted at earlier. The theme of creation out of nothing that already existed in the earlier writings has been focused in relation to the "have-nots," to those who are "lowly and nothing," in such a way as to uphold God's preferential faithfulness to poor and disregarded people like Mary. Luther interprets this concrete social referent in terms of the pervasive life situation experienced by the poor during their period of domestic servitude. The final thesis of the *Disputation*—which we argued is implicitly present in the whole of that argument—comes to explicit expression from the very beginning of this

95. LW 21.306; WA 7.553.21–554.2.
96. LW 21.297; WA 7.544.21–24.
97. LW 21.357; WA 7.602.12–14.

commentary. Rather than a tension between God and generic humanity, Luther emphasizes divisions that run through the human community and the resulting difference between God's preferential subjects and the world's. God's regard for the disregarded turns their world upside down. God's gaze is always and everywhere first directed to those who are poor, disregarded, oppressed, weak, and treated as nothing. Their reality is seen as dialectically related to the contrary group of those who are rich, honored, established, powerful, and highly valued.

In the pre-Diet section of this commentary, Luther concentrated on Mary emphasizing God's act of grace toward the poor and powerless. In the post-Diet section of the commentary, Luther moved himself into the center of the word and addressed his new concern with the particular form of oppression that he was himself experiencing. In both sections, Luther speaks of God as one who acts to raise up the lowly and bring down the mighty. Though all the world looks up and seeks to move in that direction, God's gaze is set into the depth on those who dwell there. When this gracious regard is received by the disregarded through the gift of faith, an alternative to the world's vision of the way things are is revealed. Mary and her people are suspended in a new reality where God is revealed as good and as the friend of the poor. This newly given faith offers hope to the hopeless.

A turning takes place within this document that represents a turning in the way the theology of the cross was understood. When Luther shifts his focus from the broken people like Mary toward his own plight, this mirrors an eventual shift in the movement that he leads. Luther redirects—one might even say misdirects—his theology of the cross toward the task of protecting and establishing the new theology and its movement. In this turning, a focus is lost and the good news is no longer directed primarily toward the poor. Part of the biblical commitment is sacrificed along with the poor as a narrowing, sobering and refocusing of the theology of the cross takes place. A profoundly disappointed people experience this as a betrayal of early promise that Luther showed. This is not to say that Luther abruptly stops speaking anything of relevance for those people nor that he simply becomes a lackey of the princes. Rather it is to say that a transition occurs in which much of the lively promise of the earlier period falls out of clear focus. This loss of focus occurs when Luther looks upward with the world toward those thrones that promise his movement some level of security. In this redirection of his gaze he inevitably looks away from those like Mary whom God preferentially chooses. The challenge still with us today is to recapture the lively faithfulness of the early movement. For at its best this commentary shows a deep understanding of the liberative power of God who frees an oppressed people and calls them and us all to live within a whole new order according to God's vision.

5

The Theology of the Cross in Pamphlet Form

Prelude to *The Passion of Christ and the Antichrist*

IN THE NEXT PART OF THIS CHAPTER, THE PAMPHLET *THE PASSION OF Christ and the Antichrist* will be explored. In that pamphlet, Luther's message joins forces with the artwork of Lucas Cranach the Elder. The ideas expressed in it have clear precedence in Luther's *To the Christian Nobility of the German Nation Concerning the Reform of the Christian Estate*, so that treatise will be examined first. In 1520 Luther offered his most detailed outline for reform. In it, Luther dismantled the distinction between spiritual and secular estates. The papacy had long presented the "spiritual estate" that its leadership occupied as the pinnacle of the status pyramid. Their location at the peak formed the basis of their claim to sovereignty over temporal leaders and issues. In the process of undermining this ideological and social construct, Luther offered a trenchant critique of the Roman curia based upon the witness of the word of God. Luther and Cranach's pamphlet played out these themes in illustrations and pithy statements.

In *To the German Nation*, Luther claims that the papacy has protected its privilege within three walls. If these walls were demolished, their whole enterprise would collapse. The first wall is the claim that the religious leadership are exempt from the decrees and laws made by temporal authority since God has placed the spiritual authorities over the temporal. The second wall is that the pope is the only legitimate interpreter of scripture. The final one is that only the pope can call and validate a general council of the church. The introduction to this treatise in Luther's Works correctly summarizes the impact of Luther's argument:

> In the three sections of this treatise Luther laid the ax to the
> whole complex of ideas upon which the social, political, legal
> and religious thought of the Western world had been develop-
> ing for nearly a thousand years.[1]

This grand attack waged war on the legal basis for religious domination in the political and economic life of the empire. Luther dismantled each of the three walls in turn. He wrote this critique moved by the
tyranny he had witnessed:

> It is not from sheer impertinence or rashness that I, one poor
> man, have taken it upon myself to address your worships. All
> the estates of Christendom, particularly in Germany, are now
> oppressed by distress and affliction, and this has stirred not only
> me but everybody else to cry out time and time again and to
> pray for help.[2]

The first wall, argues Luther, rests on a pure invention of Rome. In
biblical thinking, religious leaders do not form one state while princes
and peasants form another. Every walk of life is a spiritual estate or
calling. Invoking language reminiscent of his sermon on *The Blessed
Sacrament of the Holy and True Body of Christ*, Luther states that every
member is a part of the same body and no hierarchy of distinctions
is appropriate. All Christians are consecrated as priests when they are
baptized. They all share the most important elements of ministry: one
gospel, one faith, one baptism. The bishops are not set above the others but rather are set beside the others as one member within a whole
community. They do have a particular function within that community.
While their tasks are particular to the office, the authority belongs to
the whole community. Luther is so bold as to say, "Therefore, a priest in
Christendom is nothing else but an officeholder."[3] The priests are called
to the administration of word and sacrament for the sake of the whole
community. The priestly calling may be important, but so is the work
of the cobbler or the peasant. In all cases, "all the members of the body
serve one another."[4] Power should not be concentrated into a couple of

---

1. LW 44.120.
2. LW 44.124; WA 6.405.12–18.
3. LW 44.129; WA 6.408.19.
4. LW 44.130; WA 6.409.10.

hands, but should be shared since all members of the community "have like power."[5]

Luther goes so far as to claim that if a Christian community found itself prisoners in a desert and had no priest to fulfill the ministry of that office, the group need only elect one from among them to be set aside for this task. The person elected "would be as truly a priest as though he had been ordained by all the bishops and popes in the world."[6] For Luther, such a move is not only appropriate in this contrived emergency situation. This is the way every priest's consecration should be understood. The community and no single human being lifts up some in their midst to serve. God's call flows through the base, not from the top. Again, baptism fundamentally defines the Christian, nothing else. "For whoever comes out of the water of baptism can boast to be already consecrated priest, bishop, and pope."[7]

This idea has practical import. First of all, every Christian has a spiritual calling so that God's work is done by peasant, prince and faithful priest. Second, not only are the religious not superior to the secular or temporal authorities, they too must submit to the laws of the land that are executed by the temporal authorities. Priestly exemption from civil law or from taxes has no theological basis. Luther returns here to the assumptions he stated about civil life in the sermon on the sacrament: if one enjoys the benefits of citizenship, then one should also carry the responsibilities of the same. Finally, the church must be concerned about the life and wellbeing of all its members. The peasant's life is as important as the priest's. Luther laments that the official church's legal structure renders the hierarchy unable to see this:

> Moreover, it is intolerable that in canon law so much importance is attached to the freedom, life and property of the clergy, as though the laity were not also as spiritual and as good Christians as they, or did not also belong to the church. Why are your life and limb, your property and honor, so cheap and mine not, inasmuch as we are all Christians and have the same baptism, the same faith, the same Spirit, and all the rest? If a priest is murdered, the whole country is place under interdict. Why not when a peasant is murdered? How does this great dif-

5. LW 44.128; WA 6.407.30–31.
6. LW 44.128; WA 6.407.38–408.1.
7. LW 44.129; WA 6.408.11–12.

ference come about between two men who are both Christians? It comes from the laws and fabrications of men.[8]

Luther's attack on the second wall of the papal fortress flows naturally from the first one. Since baptism is consecration for ministry and through the rite all effectively are popes, no one can claim sole interpretive authority of the word for themselves. To claim this is a game of the Antichrist, the one who stands over and against Christ and his gracious gift to all. The name of Antichrist that Luther assigns to the pope multiple times in this treatise will be picked up as the organizing principle of *The Passion of Christ and of the Antichrist*. Luther stands against the tyranny. He quotes Paul to show that all Christians are given the "mind of Christ" and thus are called to interpret his word. Luther exhorts his fellow believers, "We ought not to allow the Spirit of freedom ... to be frightened off by the fabrications of the popes, but we ought to march boldly forward and test all that they do ..."[9]

"The third wall falls of itself when the first two are down."[10] Without a privileged place in the sole spiritual estate and without exclusive interpretive powers, the idea that the pope alone could purify the church through a council is rejected easily. This has no scriptural warrant and even contradicts the realities of how past councils were called.

Luther has attacked the foundation of papal ideology in the law. "We could never fathom the arbitrary will of the pope, which is all that canon law has become."[11] The law has come in to do its vicious work of establishing papal privilege. Especially, the law has been destructive of the community in the juridical quest to increase Rome's resources. "O what assessing and fleecing goes on there! It seems as though canon law were instituted solely for the purpose of making money."[12] Luther's raging against the pope also turns to those who have joined forces with him. He personifies the pope as Greed or Avarice and states, "Since this boundless Avarice is not satisfied with all this wealth, wealth with which three great kings would be content, he now begins to transfer this

---

8. LW 44.132; WA 6.410.11–17.

9. LW 44.135; WA 6.412.26–29.

10. LW 44.136; WA 6.413.1.

11. LW 44.203; WA 6.459.20–21.

12. LW 44.154; WA 6.426.10–12.

trade and sell it to the Fuggers of Augsburg."[13] He goes on to condemn the way ecclesiastic and economic powers have ruined the life of both church and country. Later when he suggests specific reforms, Luther calls for someone to reign in those who like the Fuggers make money off another's labors or misery. The concern that Luther had was not only the corruption that their dealings brought to the church, but also the harm that it causes to all who are vulnerable to its pursuits. Profits, together with the unrestrained quest for power and prestige, bring violence and injustice down unto his beloved Germany.

> There is buying, selling, bartering, changing, trading, drunkenness, lying, deceiving, robbing, stealing, luxury, harlotry, knavery, and every sort of contempt of God [in the affairs of Rome]. Even the rule of the Antichrist could not be more scandalous.[14]

These walls must fall, says Luther, for they have led to selective faithfulness and sporadic ministry. "The pope is a shepherd, but only so long as you have money, and no longer."[15]

Luther has demolished the legal edifice of papal privilege. In the process of creating this rubble, Luther often contrasts the pope and his lifestyle with that of Jesus. Above all else, these contradictions inspire *The Passion of Christ and of the Antichrist*. Luther, for example, accused the pope of wishing to be a vicar of Christ glorified in heaven rather than of Christ crucified.[16] The pope wishes to rule from on high like Christ seated at God's right hand. Power defines the pope's rule. Luther would have them learn from Jesus the nature of their office. In images now familiar to us, Luther calls the church back to the cross in order to stand in service to the neighbor at hand. But this would require a new mind, for they:

> turn all that upside down. They take the heavenly and kingly form of Christ and give it to the pope, and leave the form of a servant to perish completely. He might almost be the Counter-Christ, whom the Scriptures call Antichrist, for all his nature,

---

13. LW 44.155; WA 6.426.25–38.
14. LW 44.153; WA 6.425.19–22.
15. LW 44.188; WA 6.449.30–31.
16. LW 44.140; WA 6.416.7–8.

work, and pretensions run counter to Christ and only blot out Christ's nature and destroy his work.[17]

The signs of this infatuation with glory are apparent for any who look upon the pope. "He [the pope] wears a triple crown, whereas the highest monarchs wear but one. If that is like the poverty of Christ and of St. Peter, then it is a new and strange kind of likeness!"[18] This becomes for Luther a symbol of the pope's political interests. These interests contaminate the pope's ministry. In regards to the *Donation of Constantine* upon which Rome based its sovereignty over the temporal authorities Luther states:

> How can a man rule and at the same time preach, pray, study and care for the poor? Yet these are the duties which most properly and peculiarly belong to the pope, and they were so earnestly imposed by Christ that he even forbade his disciples to take cloak or money with them.[19]

Against this attitude Luther calls the pope back to simple faithfulness:

> The pope should not allow his court to surpass the courts of all kings in pomp and extravagance, because this kind of thing not only has never been of any use to the cause of the Christian faith, but has kept the courtesans from study and prayer until they are hardly able to speak about faith at all.[20]

How do these worldly pretensions relate to Christ? Luther states, "Even Christ, whose vicar the pope boasts he is, was never willing to have anything to do with temporal rule."[21]

Together with the drive for political power, the pope's quest for pomp and privilege reveals him as Contra-Christ. Take his mode of transportation:

> Another example of the same scandalous pride is that the pope is not satisfied to ride or be driven, but, although he is strong and in good health, he has himself borne by men like an idol and with unheard-of splendor. Dear readers, how does such sa-

17. LW44.165; WA 6.434.13–17.
18. LW 44.139–40; WA 6.415.23–25.
19. LW 44.166; WA 6.434.29–33.
20. LW 44.163; WA 6.432.26–31.
21. LW 44.167–68; WA 6.435.19–20.

tanic pride compare with Christ, who went on foot, as did all
his disciples?[22]

Finally, not only does the pope, unlike Christ, seek prestige, rather
he runs from legitimate practice of servanthood.

> Christ washed his disciples' feet and dried them but the disci-
> ples never washed his feet [John 13:4–16]. The pope, as though
> he were higher than Christ, turns that about and allows his feet
> to be kissed as a great favor.[23]

The theme of "volatile knowledge" from the *Heidelberg Disputation*
comes across clearly in this writing. Through "violence and unjust
means" the pope robs others of their proper authority.[24] Luther recalled
the particular violence of Pope Julius II, whose rule ended a few years
before the Reformation began. The popes who confuse themselves with
royalty and wage vicious wars are "princes of hell. These princes could
fill the world with war and bloodshed. . . ."[25] Luther called for his people
to demonstrate a different kind of understanding that is not founded
upon violence and threats. He continued, "war and bloodshed do not
overcome [the princes of hell]. We must tackle this job by renouncing
trust in physical force and trust humbly in God."[26]

Just as Luther had linked the pope to evil using the language of
Antichrist, he also spoke of the papacy as bound for hell. Luther declared, "Hear this, O pope, not of all men the holiest but of all men the
most sinful! O that God from heaven would soon destroy your throne
and sink it in the abyss of hell!"[27] The pope has usurped not only the
rule of temporal authorities, but also that of God. He has replaced God's
generous gifts with shoddy wares sold at high prices.

> The fact is the pope leads you away from the gifts of God, which
> are yours without cost, to his gifts, for which you have to pay.
> He gives you lead for gold, the letter for the spirit. You see all
> this before your very eyes, but you refuse to take notice. If you
> intend to ride to heaven on his wax and parchment, this chariot

22. LW 44.168–69; WA 6.436.10–14. cf. LW 44.147; WA 6.424.25–27.

23. LW 44.168; WA 6.435.29–33.

24. LW 44.209; WA 6.463.26.

25. LW 44.125; WA 6.406.7–8.

26. LW 44.125–26; WA 6.8–11.

27. LW 44.193; WA 6.453.10–14.

will soon break down and you will fall into hell, and not in God's name!"[28]

This image will close out the pamphlet as it raises up drawings in the hopes that those who "refuse to take notice" will finally see. Luther chastised a church leadership that had sought after other gods. His critique could be summarized with this sentence from the treatise, "They do not seek to save souls, but, like all the pope's henchmen, only their own power, profit, and prestige."[29]

The Passion of Christ and of the Antichrist

The following year Luther wrote the text for a series of twenty-six woodcuts drawn by Lucas Cranach the Elder. A translated copy of this pamphlet and its images can be found in the appendix of this book. Take a moment and look at the images. With a strong thesis/antithesis style to rival his *Heidelberg Disputation*, the faith, life and commitments of the papacy are placed along side of Jesus' practice. What Luther invoked several times in *To the Christian Nobility*, he and Cranach make into their organizing principle. Thus with Jesus and the pope juxtaposed, the creators make clear the explicit divergences that had occurred between the passion of Christ and the passion of the "Antichrist." Luther's commentary in *The German Nation* appears in an abbreviated form with illustrations; it is like a series of political cartoons. The use of this pamphlet in the work of propagating the Reformation was powerful due to the fact that one need not even read the accompanying text to get a sense of the critique offered. Illiterate people were engaged visually by the dramatic differences between the primitive Christian movement and the contemporary church's corruption.

For those who could read, however, another of Luther's points came in the form of the text. The short paragraphs that accompanied the Christ side of the dialectic were quotations of scriptural texts. The short paragraphs that accompanied the papal or Antichrist drawings were based on declarations from canon law. Thus the authority of papal tradition was shown to have digressed from scripture and was built upon a human contrivance.

28. LW 44.189; WA 6.450.11–13.
29. LW44.197; WA 6.455.19–20.

This pamphlet shows the direction that Luther understood his message to be moving in relation to the common people. In pamphlet form Luther's message translated into a medium one step closer to the common people of his day than even his German sermons. In this pamphlet, the life and ministry of Jesus is brought to bear as a trenchant critique on the ecclesiastical leadership of the day. The combination of visual images and written text attack the power, prestige, profits, and pomp of the papacy.

What is most striking about these drawings is the contrast between the simple life of humility and service chosen by Jesus and the ostentatious quest for power, profit, and prestige chosen by the papacy. As in the *Heidelberg Disputation*, Luther makes the accusation, this time visually, that the leaders of the church seek good only in glory and majesty and thus not in the lowliness and disgrace of crosses and passions. As in the *Heidelberg Disputation* this location has the double meaning of both Christ's cross and humanity's suffering and oppression. The Roman authorities do not seek God in Christ, and thus in these drawings no continuity can be claimed between their mode of life and that of Christ's. But also they do not seek to locate themselves in the place of lowliness and disgrace. Whereas the depictions of Jesus in these drawings regularly place him along side of the poor and suffering people, the depictions of the papacy either exclude representation of the common people altogether or demonstrate how they are present only when they serve papal interests, for example, paying indulgences. In the case of Jesus, service flows out of him toward the people; in the case of the pope, all servants bow before his own needs and desires.

This pamphlet displays a broad understanding of "passion." The whole life of Jesus is understood as his passion and is revelatory of the way that God wills to be present in a situation of division. Only a third of the events shown in the drawings are from the "passion" week drama: the entrance into Jerusalem, the cleansing of the temple, the washing of feet, the crowning with thorns and the carrying of his cross. Amazingly, the first editions of *The Passion of Christ and the Antichrist* had no scenes that included the cross! In a slightly later edition included in this book, Christ carries his cross in one of the frames. Originally this sixth pair contrasted Christ's barefooted walking with the pope's transportation in splendor. Then a later edition made the wise move to a sharpened contrast by portraying Christ who carried his cross with the pope who is carried in splendor. The lack of depiction of the cross itself is not an indication that the concrete cross of Jesus did not matter, but that the whole life of Jesus lived in service to those who suffer is what is rightly called his passion. From his birth in a manger to his proclamation to his healing of the poor, Christ demonstrated the way that the theologian of the cross lives. The cross is but the logical ending to his cruciform life.

The first pair of images sets the tone for the entire pamphlet. Christ does not seek power for himself, but rather declares that the one who wishes to be great must serve the least; the pope, on the other hand, seeks to fortify his power. Canon law claims to give him "unquestionable supremacy...over the empire" as the text indicates, but the law is buttressed by cannons of a military sort flanked by a host of armed soldiers. This is a clear depiction of the convergence of intellectual power (canon law) and actual violence (cannons) that Luther called volatile knowledge in the *Heidelberg Disputation*. The pope bears the sign of this convergence, the triple crown. Not only Jesus, but Peter from whom the popes claim their legitimacy, offers criticism of the circumstances, "There will come impudent bishops who despise the earthly authorities."

This headgear claims the focus of the next pair. Christ is shown being beaten as he is crowned with thorns; the pope, however, sits on a throne surrounded by luxury as he is crowned with the triple tiara. "Finery" and "tyranny" mark his reign. Throughout the rest of this series of drawings the pope wears the crown as a sign of political power while Christ goes forth with head bare. Through the opening to the left of this drawing, one sees again cannons blazing and armed men shooting their weapons in the opposite direction of the pope toward a hidden enemy. The target is not seen, although visually it is the Christ whose drawing lies to the left. The text refers to the *Donation of Constantine* with the biting commentary, "In order to preserve their tyranny they have put forth lies like this ..."

The next pair begins with Jesus exercising leadership by washing and even kissing his disciples' feet. Jesus is bowed down before those whom he serves. His voice is heard through the text as he points out the importance of his act to them. They are to act among themselves as Christ has acted toward them. In stark contrast to this, the pope is shown as "presumptuous" seated on his throne with the emperor bowed before him in a posture that mirrors that of Jesus. The pope places himself above even the highest authorities in the land, while Jesus serves the lowly. The text makes the connection to the Antichrist clear: "Whoever does not worship the image of this beast is to be killed. Apocalypse 13:15."

In the next set, the disgust over clergy exemption from local taxes draws the viewer's anger toward the papacy. Jesus finds a way to pay his requisite taxes, while the pope places a ban over those who would extract taxes from monks and nuns. Notice that the theme of obedience to authority from Romans 13 is used in this pairing not as an injunction against rebellion by the oppressed but rather as a denunciation of clergy privilege. The text links this to the notion of secular and spiritual estates that Luther rejected in *To the German Nation*.

With whom will one enter into solidarity? This issue is raised in the next set of pictures. Christ stands among the poor and destitute bringing healing. The pope occupies the highest place in the corresponding picture as tournament knights—certainly not symbolic of healing—bow before him. The left hand text invokes the hymn from Philippians 2 that speaks of the divine Christ assuming the form of a farmhand, slave, or vassal. Christ stood among the people as one of them. The pope took the inverse option, seeking his own honor and refusing to humble himself. If one were to think that the knights were merely present as sportsmen for the tournament, the text speaks of other motives. "It is necessary to govern the German fools harshly" so that they learn to show proper honor to the pope. The polemic is poignant. Christ draws near to the people to bring them health and wellbeing; the pope draws together military personnel to bring threats to the German people with profits and honor rising to himself.

The following set of drawings appears in two versions depending upon the edition of the pamphlet one consults. As stated earlier, the first edition of the pamphlet contrasts the barefooted travels of Jesus and his disciples with the splendor of the pope's mode of transport in the papal litter. Later editions sharpen the distinction by contrasting the pope who is carried in splendor with the Christ who carries his own instrument of execution, the cross. In the drawing of Jesus, he is surrounded by and threatened with the very weapons so prevalent in the other drawings as the protectors of papal privilege. The weapons that protect the pope attack Christ. Christ's command to take up the cross provides part of the caption on Jesus' side of the pamphlet. This is contrasted with the pope who is unwilling "to bear the cross of offense:

he damns and hands over to the devil any who lay a hand on the priests." With sarcasm Luther states, "the Pope 'bears' the cross: that baptized Christians have to carry *him* on their shoulders!" How unlike Christ shouldering the tremendous burden on his way to Golgotha!

The themes of alliances and honor are again invoked in the next drawings. Christ stands before the common people preaching the gospel. He proclaims that he has no other option since "for I was sent for this purpose." Meanwhile, the pope and his bishops gorge on rich foods as musicians entertain them. Their luxurious lifestyle keeps them from their proper task of preaching the gospel to the people. They are overwhelmed with the tasks of enjoying themselves and engaging in warfare. Luther puts Isaiah's quotation regarding other unfaithful leaders on their lips, "Come, let's feast and make merry, and enjoy the good life forever!" The gospel of Christ announced to the common people is contrasted with the self-indulgence of the papacy that has led him to forget the proclamation of the gospel.

The next pairing begins with the humble origins of Jesus born in a stable as a sign of the life he would continue to live. Two biblical citations reinforce this point. The first is from Luke 9 where Jesus notes that he has no place to lay his head. The second is from 2 Corinthians 8, "This one, although he was rich, nevertheless for our sakes became poor, and his poverty has made us rich." This option for solidarity with the poor and the taking on of their social location is contrasted with the pope decked out in battle array and surrounded by soldiers and weaponry. They are ready to protect clergy property at any cost. Spears and a cannon, soldiers and property fill the visual frame to the point of bursting. The text again challenges the two estates division. Luther also cites the promise of the pope that "whoever dies or is ruined in this war shall attain eternal life." The wages of war earn one an eternal victory. Not Christ's blood, but the soldier's goods bring him to heaven.

This kind of contrast is continued in the next set of drawings as Christ humbly enters Jerusalem surrounded by common people. The text mentions that Christ does not come to impose his rule, but to give us eternal life. The pope comes riding on a stallion, led by foot soldiers, and traveling to hell. He tries even to make the emperor into his servant. The tenth pair continues the polemic against wealth and the distancing from the poor that accompanies greed. Christ commands his followers to denounce worldly possessions. The pope proudly displays to a bishop the wealth of the city. The text on the left recalls Peter's words "I have neither gold nor silver" and asks, "Where then is St. Peter's heritage?" Clearly not in the Vatican where, we are told, papal decree disallows the consecration of a bishop in a small or poor town that would not properly provide for him. Again, wealth drives a wedge between the institutional church hierarchy and the poor.

The following drawings pick up on a different Reformation theme. True worship, simple and humble, is contrasted with the external pomp and trappings of papal ceremony. In the left hand drawing the simple disciples prepare to celebrate the Lord's Supper at its institution; the pomp and regalia of the right hand drawing demonstrate the interests of erring, opulent religion. It is all about "externals" that glorify the clergy as though "laity were not the Church nor of God."

In the penultimate pairing, Christ angrily drives the moneychangers out of Temple. In the right hand drawing the pope sits behind a money changing table signing indulgences. Reference is again made to the pope as Antichrist. The implication is that Christ stands against those who have again turned God's holy place into a house of profiteering. This has been an important theme for the theology of the cross since the *Ninety-five Theses*. The pope is interested in bringing affliction to the people and gathering treasures to himself. For Christ said, "You received it free of charge, therefore give it free of charge." If not, "May your money go with you into damnation!" The pope has confused himself with God, but even in that confusion acts nothing like the true God who graciously gives to all.

The final pair of drawings render God's verdict over the two ways of being in the world. Christ ascends into heaven where he is welcomed by angels. The pope, ceremoniously dressed and still wearing the triple crown, is thrown into hell's fire where he is welcomed by demons. God executes the final judgment.

Several themes that are worthy of note in relation to the theology of the cross have been portrayed in this work. First of all, the cross and passion marked the whole life of Jesus including his birth, his ministry with the poor, and the events with which his life culminated. A theme of two convergences already detected in the earlier writings are clarified and perhaps even intensified through visual portrayal. The first convergences is that the option to pursue wealth and honor leads to a corresponding retreat from life lived with and for the poor. In the extravagant world of papal luxury, the poor cannot be seen. The worldly pursuits of the papacy are contrasted with the way of Christ wherein he became poor for the sake of others. The human pretensions critiqued are not generic human assertion over and against God, but rather the particular pretensions of one segment of humanity over and against both God and the common people.

The second convergence with the earlier theology of the cross is the theme of volatile knowledge. In this pamphlet, canon law comes together with cannon fire, both equally deadly in their effects. Pretentious papal knowledge and rights established and protected, together with its other interests, by manipulation of the law and military might. The omnipresence of weaponry in the Antichrist drawings provides a striking critique of this reality. Throughout these drawings graphic depictions of the papacy portray it as bent on its own pomp, power, prestige, and profits. God in Christ is depicted as being with the poor even though this entails a flight from pomp, power, prestige, and profits. The judgment of God against the pope is definitive in the final drawing. Your ways are not my ways; this is the end you seek!

The visual images together with the texts present the theology of the cross in a particularly concrete and specific way. What is more, they do this with an eye toward reaching the people to whom Jesus had dedicated his ministry. The message of the theology of the cross is movingly appropriate when translated into the most popular of media of this day. For the Christ who is depicted in illustrations as for the poor, actually comes through pictures to those poor who cannot read in order to reveal God's solidarity with them. Medium and message reinforce each other in dedication to those who know crosses and suffering as a constant companion.

6

Luther's Theology of the Cross in Jeopardy

HAVING LOOKED AT THE THEOLOGY OF THE CROSS AS IT APPEARED in the early years of the Reformation, and having claimed that Luther moves away from central aspects of his early confessional stance, we now must examine two writings that Luther wrote in 1525, *The Bondage of the Will* and *Against the Robbing and Murdering Hordes of Peasants.*

The Bondage of the Will

The first of these is one of Luther's most intellectually challenging writings. In regard to its relationship with the theology of the cross, it remains one of the most controversial. Some interpreters such as Forde see this treatise as the most faithful renderings of the theology of cross. Others such as Loewenich see it as a contradiction of the theology of the cross.

Luther wrote this treatise in response to the work of the humanist author Desiderius Erasmus. Erasmus claimed that humans possess a power of the will by which a person can apply him or herself toward gaining eternal salvation.[1] Luther responded with a brutal attack on both the eloquent author and his ideas:

> . . . your book struck me as so cheap and paltry that I felt profoundly sorry for you, defiling as you were your very elegant and ingenious style with such trash, and quite disgusted at the utterly unworthy matter that was being conveyed in such ornaments of eloquence, like filth or crap being carried in gold and silver vases.[2]

1. Erasmus, *Discourse on Free Will.*
2. LW 33.16; WA 18.601.7–11.

Luther insisted that the human will is absolutely enslaved and that one cannot do anything whatsoever to contribute in the least to salvation. In this thing that is above human capability, God works all in all. The will is never free, that is, guided by some power in human nature. Satan rides human beings like beasts of burden making them go where he wishes. Only when God comes in mercy does that beast do an about face. But it is still the rider that matters, not the beast! Yes, a kind of freedom appears to our eyes when the Holy Spirit does its work and guides a person in holy living; yet it is a strange thing to call this freedom, for "through his Spirit we are again slaves and captives—though this is a royal freedom—so that we readily will and do what he wills."[3] Luther appropriately throws the whole promise of salvation onto the work of Christ through the Holy Spirit. In this sense, this writing is priceless and deserves Luther's own appraisal of it as one of his finest works. Yet just as Luther claimed throughout this treatise that Erasmus' own arguments come out against him, so too Luther makes assertions that not only contradict each other but also jeopardize his whole proclamation.

Luther used terminology that at first sounds familiar: God is hidden, God is revealed. The revealed God is the key to the Christian life. In Jesus Christ, God comes out to humanity as pure grace and love. Luther calls for extreme attentiveness to God's mercy as it is made known in Christ Jesus. Speaking of this, Luther states, "For it is this that God as he is preached is concerned with, namely that sin and death should be taken away and we should be saved. For 'he sent his word and healed them' [Ps. 107: 20]."[4] This preached God must not be lost from sight or the Christian shall be lost. "Take Christ out of the Scriptures, and what will you find left of them?"[5] asked Luther. The implied response is nothing . . . or worse, one may be left with nothing but unchecked wrath. So far, so good. But then in a way uncharacteristic of his earlier work where God was hidden in the crucified Christ, and therefore hiddenness and suffering corresponded, now the hiddenness of God is severed from the cross. The hiddenness becomes utter mystery that defines divinity in terms of power alone. Rather than divine hiddenness in cross and suffering providing an epistemological key to the very being of God

3. LW 33.65; WA 18.635.15–18.
4. LW 33.140; WA 18.685.19–21.
5. LW 33.26; WA 18.606.29.

and reality, now another possibility exists. The God we preach in Christ is merciful, but beyond or behind that one there may be another that utterly contradicts the crucified revelation. Mercy may not win the day, but may be overcome by the hidden and awful will of God. God locked away in divine majesty is terrifying power binding himself to nothing and controlling all things under the sway of his omnipotence. This "God hidden in his majesty neither deplores nor takes away death, but works life, death, and all in all. *For there he has not bound himself by his word, but has kept himself free over all things.*"[6]

This move on Luther's part threatens to undo the whole promise of the gospel. What has Luther discovered if not that God is as good as God's word and that word is Jesus? While God could have chosen to act otherwise, God in Christ has chosen to be bound to and by the word revealed in the crucified Christ. God has declared, "This is the kind of God I am and I will be no other." God's self-limitation is real and is the source of Christian hope. Luther has forgotten that the preached God, naked and dying on the cross, is the hidden God, hidden from what we would ever expect given human infatuation with power, prestige, and profits. God Godself is hidden in the cross not because God is absent, but because human eyes refuse to believe that God could be present in such places.

To Luther's credit, he only speaks of the hidden God in order to warn all not to go there. He calls the faithful to go where God is clothed and preached as mercy. But though Luther insists that one cannot know about the God hidden and utterly free in mystery, he himself assumes a great deal about that God. The unseen God is defined as absolute power and control, one who works all things and causes things to happen just as they do by divine necessity. This God is indistinguishable from "Fate" as Luther himself argues bringing the Greek poets in to support his claim that this is what God is like.[7]

Luther has not left the awful God alone, but has set him to work to wreak havoc in the world. While Luther's claim that "the operations of God are not . . . bourgeois"[8] is provocative, the omnipotent God who has set the world up as it is and maintains it in this way through the

6. Emphasis mine, LW 33.140; WA 18.685.23–25.
7. LW 33.41; WA 18.617.25f.
8. LW 33.54; WA 18.627.18.

temporal sword is incredibly bourgeois. The powerful God comes out not with Mary but on the side of the world's thrones and dominions to "restrain" the "common people."[9] God and tyrants are birds of a feather, in spite of what the powerful did to the crucified Christ. The practical implications of Luther's claims will be examined shortly in his tract against the rebelling peasants.

Much of what was essential in the early theology of the cross has shifted radically with time. The kind of enslavement explained concretely as Mary's enslavement to a system of dishonor, or as human enslavement to greed and selfishness in the sermon on the Lord's supper, or as enslavement to papal power, prestige, pomp, and profits in the pamphlet literature yields again in this Latin opus to the more abstract and generic notion of the enslavement of the will.

Luther wished to make a truth claim about God, and this is not merely a tactic. In the end, one must recognize with Luther that the concept of the enslaved will attacks all pretensions, whether those of humans in general or specifically of theologians. And this is not its final destiny. The enslavement of the will is not simply something about humans; ultimately, it is a faithful confession and safeguarding of God's graciousness. It is important in the final instance to assert that humans are enslaved in order to bring to light the utter graciousness that occurs when God sets them free. Christ alone brings freedom from bondage. The doctrine of the bound will ultimately must be understood as doxological. It defines God as unilateral liberator. It properly indicates that the work of salvation is done from God's side and that humans have nothing to contribute to this thing "above us." In this sense, I make no objection to the concept.

Yet, this is not the only way that the doctrine functions in this opus. Whereas properly understood, the doctrine directs the reader to the all graciousness of God hidden in the cross of Christ, in this writing, Luther pushes beyond this intent in a way that nearly undoes his proper confession. The theology of the cross in the early years of the Reformation was a tool for confronting the volatile power encoded in the theology of the institutional church. Luther confronted the church with a vision of God that totally upset its understanding of God. He pointed toward the crucified Christ and claimed that the cross alone was to be our theology.

9. LW 33.49; WA 624.13.

By doing this, God was defined fundamentally in terms of suffering and the cross over and against the dominant theology that defined God in relation to power. The justifying mercy of God challenged all claims to the contrary. God was hidden in the cross as an unexpected, unnoticed, and even despised, divine presence. Not only was God hidden in the cross, but also in the crosses and passions that human beings suffer. The promises of God were hidden, for example, under Mary's lowly exterior. In the earlier writings, hiddenness corresponds with the actual presence of God in suffering and the cross. Though in such places we see the *backside* of God, it is nonetheless the backside of *God*. As such it threatens any systematic thinking that equates God with power and prestige. Through this disguised presence, God breaks what is established and establishes what is broken. God has bound Godself to the crucified Christ in such a way that this cannot be undone.

By the time Luther writes *The Bondage of the Will*, the hiddenness of God itself becomes a systematic concept and absorbs meanings foreign to the original usage. While Luther continued his injunctions against gazing at God in majesty and power, he also came to assert that power and majesty in the guise of omnipotence is nevertheless the defining characteristic of God. God is no longer hidden in suffering and the cross, but now is completely hidden, even absent, during the act of revelation itself so that the God totally hidden from view could conceivably override the gracious and merciful revelation that is present in sufferings and the cross. Sheer power rather than sheer grace may ultimately define God. The totally hidden God may be the antithesis of the God revealed in a hidden way in the crucified Christ. The revelation on the cross may not define God at all! God may take back God's word of promise and become the very antithesis of the one whom we know in Christ crucified. The solidarity of God and God's gracious regard for the disregarded is jeopardized in favor of a God who may not befriend the powerless but may himself be the apex of the arbitrary use of absolute power. No longer is the glory of God found in the saving of those who like Mary are despised and rejected nor in pulling the powerful from their thrones. Now the glory of God is to be celebrated even if God is thought to damn the world. No longer does Luther claim that God always and only recreates those who are seen as nothing by the world; now perhaps God would join the world in its attack upon the despised, wretched peoples of the earth. The certainty and comfort that Luther wished to sow has been uprooted by his new claims. McGrath is correct when he states:

> This argument inevitably makes theology an irrelevancy, if any statements which can be made on the basis of divine revelation may be refuted by appealing to a hidden and inscrutable God, whose will probably contradicts that of the revealed God. . . . His dilemma is his own creation, and his failure to resolve it in *de servo arbitrio* an indication of his abandonment of his own principle: *Crux sola nostra theologia!*[10]

Against the Robbing and Murdering Hordes of Peasants

This move toward the systemic confession of God as unlimited power is asserted in the same year that Luther himself calls for a volatile response to the peasant uprisings that were occurring at the time. Luther's explosive reaction to the peasants surprised many of them. In fact, at least on two occasions prior to Luther's public responses, the peasants had appealed to him as an arbitrator in their case, a sure sign that they were confident that he would take their side. Luther attacked them on three accounts. First, they had broken their oath of submission and obedience to government officials. Secondly, they had robbed and plundered goods that were not theirs. Finally, they had dishonored God's name by dragging it through the devil's service in this act of rebellion. Having accused the peasants of picking up a sword that does not belong to them by divine right, he then viciously invites anyone and everyone to claim such authority for themselves against the peasants. He called out, "let everyone who can smite, slay, and stab, secretly or openly, remembering that nothing can be more poisonous, hurtful, or devilish than a rebel."[11] Luther argues that the peasants have confused the gospel that relates to the soul with issues of bodily freedom and property.

Luther then addressed the authorities. If a ruler is not a Christian, "I will not oppose a ruler who, even though he does not tolerate the gospel, will smite and punish these peasants without first offering to submit the case to judgment."[12] The rebels are guilty without the benefit of any

---

10. McGrath, *Luther's Theology of the Cross*, 167.
11. LW 46.50; WA 18.358.14–16.
12. LW 46.52; WA 18.359.14–15.

trial. He commanded the rulers to destroy the peasants and thus acted as an unwitting servant of his glorious God who acts in divine wrath.

For Christian rulers the matter is more complex. They should confess that this rebellion is indeed just divine punishment for Germany. Second, they should pray "for help against the devil."[13] Third, above and beyond the call of duty, they should offer the "mad peasants" an opportunity to come to terms.[14] But, "Finally, if that does not help, then swiftly take to the sword."[15] They should go about their bloody work quickly. "This is not the time to sleep. And there is no place for patience or mercy. This is the time of the sword, not the day of grace."[16] Luther offers a prayer that rulers might raise to God, recognizing that the failure to wield the sword will mean a forfeiting of divine grace! The ruler should end the prayer with a stirring promise to God, "I will punish and smite as long as my heart beats."[17]

Luther himself seems to have profound problems separating that which pertains to the "soul" from that which pertains to the "body." He presents his own theology of glory in the face of what he perceives as the peasants' theology of glory. Through wielding the sword one might become a "true martyr in the eyes of God . . ."[18] Indeed, these "are strange times, when a prince can win heaven with bloodshed better than others with prayer!"[19] How odd to hear Luther speak of anyone doing anything to win heaven! His revulsion at revolt is so strong his language slips into complete denial of his most fundamental principle. They are saved through works, specifically works of violence. Love of neighbor is no longer called for, but stabbing, smiting and slaying as an act of mercy for these poor people. In fact, his own claim here sounds like the very one he condemned in the *Passion of Christ and of the Antichrist*. There, as you may recall, Luther chastised the promise of the pope that "whoever dies or is ruined in this war shall attain eternal life."

---

13. LW 46.52; WA 18.359.31.
14. LW 46.52; WA 18.359.35–36.
15. LW 46.52; WA 18.359.31.
16. LW 46.53; WA 18.360.10–11.
17. LW 46.53; WA 18.360.26–27.
18. LW 46.53; WA 18.360.28–29.
19. LW 46.54; WA 18.361.4–6.

Luther's move toward defining God in terms of power and allow-ing the hidden God to act in a way contrary to the preached God had deadly effects in this fateful year. The early enthusiasm expressed by the poor for the gospel that Luther proclaimed was slain. Luther, who had once stood for a symbol of liberation for the common German people, now was seen as their betrayer. The Mayor of Zwickau wrote to Stephen Roth of the change in Luther's popularity, "Doctor Martin has fallen into great disfavor with the common people . . . having been too fickle . . . [Luther chose to be] the hammer of the poor, without regard for their need, by calling for the poor alone to be quickly destroyed."[20] One could hardly blame them for feeling betrayed. Roughly one hun-dred thousand peasants were slaughtered in the violent response of the authorities.[21] In the beginning of the Reformation the gospel stood with the poor against the established church; now Luther proclaimed the omnipotent God with the enthroned powers who stood with Luther to establish the legitimacy of his own church. While one might charitably note Luther's call for patience and his harsh words offered to the rul-ers in other documents, it is unrealistic to expect that the blessing he gave to their bloodshed would not be seized upon. An overwhelming, all-consuming shadow of divine dominance has been cast over the cru-cified God. A betrayal has occurred from which the Reformation never recovers!

20. Hermann Mühlpoft's letter to Stephan Roth at Wittenberg. 4 June 1525 in Scribner, *The German Peasants' War: A History in Documents*, 322.

21. Blickle, *The Revolution of 1525*, 165.

7

The Vocation of the Theologian of the Cross

HAVING LOOKED AT HOW LUTHER INSERTED HIS THOUGHT INTO THE power relationships of his day, general observations about his early theology of the cross can now be made. How do theologians of the cross faithfully fulfill their vocation? These theses are drawn critically and respectfully from Luther's work, but will also move toward a constructive proposal for being a theologian of the cross in our own day. At key moments these theses ask about the theologian's practice of doing theology in a social context, and not merely the formal or conceptual dimensions of his or her theology. In this way, they differ from Loewenich's five dimensions of the theology of the cross while still being highly influenced by them.

1. Theologians of the cross live and think in a way that is centered in Christ crucified as the definitive, though hidden, revelation of God.

For Luther, the knowledge of God is hidden but indeed present in the crucified Christ. The *Heidelberg Disputation* made this claim most succinctly when it stated, "In Christ crucified is true theology and knowledge of God."[1] Luther's writings abound with the insight that God is known most radically in the midst of the suffering and lowliness seen in the cross. In the highly conflictive situation of the indulgence controversy, Luther called on a complacent and distant church leadership to count suffering as God most precious gift. This suffering and lowliness is not confined to the cross upon which Jesus was executed, but is also the mark of Jesus' whole life beginning with his birth into a poor family.

---

1. Trans. mine, cf. LW 31.53; WA 1.362.18–19.

Having been carried by God's chosen one, Mary, the unwed domestic worker, devoid of earthly power, pomp or wealth, Jesus lived with the lowly as one of them. Likewise his own death summed up the life he had lived. God chooses this route to be with humanity because God wishes to be known and worshipped hidden in suffering. This understanding of "hiddenness" in the very act of revelation is Luther's fundamental one, rather than the total hiddenness of God apart from Christ.

This revelation occurs not only in the location of Christ's cross on Golgotha, but also in the crosses born by humanity. God chooses to be hidden in human sufferings and crosses, in the lowliness and disgrace of the poor. In the *Magnificat* we heard Luther exclaim, "What great things are hidden under this lowly exterior!"[2] He referred, of course, to Mary. The poor domestic servant is the place of divine revelation. Mary and those like her reveal God hidden in suffering and their own passion (*passionibus*). This theme was also present in the *Blessed Sacrament of the Holy and True Body of Christ*. The complete solidarity of God with marginalized people demands that theologians of the cross, and by this we mean *all* Christians, look toward the poor. For those unwilling to do this, Christ is not salvifically present; those who refuse to look toward those members who are in need have no place in the assembly. Finally, this theme is graphically portrayed in the *Passion of Christ and of the Antichrist* where Jesus is continually found among the poor, disrespected and rejected people. He in fact becomes one of them. It is quite interesting that the aspect of hiddenness in concrete human disgrace is most powerful in the work that Luther oriented toward popular audiences. This theme appears in sermons, devotional tracts, and finally pamphlets that Luther created for German Marys rather than for scholars in debate!

All this suggests that for Luther the theology of the cross was first and foremost about our way of knowing. While the cross undoubtedly has soteriological and ethical dimensions, for the theologian of the cross it functions primarily to give shape to what Mary Solberg has gracefully called an "epistemology of the cross."[3] Where do we look in order to understand God, creation, and our place in the world? Do we look toward safe and secure places at the center of power? Do we proclaim

---

2. LW 21.329; WA 7.575.23–24.

3. Solberg, *Compelling Knowledge*, 17.

in comfort, "Peace, peace" where there is no peace?[4] Or do recognize the margins not as a world apart, but as the gage revealing the health of the whole system? If you want to know about the wellbeing of the church in Luther's Germany, do not sit content at an Archbishop's dinner table, slip into the kitchen and have a chat with his domestic servant Mary. Without Mary, her labor, and her exploitation, the splendid table could not and would not be set. In fact, in light of this reality the splendid table may not be so splendid after all.

For Luther, the papal exploitation of Germany not only caused vicious deterioration in his own country, it explained the rampant decadence of Rome itself. As Westhelle states, "the margin is not the weak side of society, but rather the place where the fragility of the whole society is manifested. It is for this reason that any institutionalized society must hide its margin, to avoid the exposing of its own fragility."[5] Thus Luther raises questions about how the abuse of the German margins by the Roman center is but a manifestation of the ecclesial propensity to occult its own fragility, inadequacy, or sinfulness. The violent force aimed at Germany sought to divert attention from the utter impotency of the church as it stood before God.

2. Since theologians of the cross live and think in a way that is centered in Christ crucified as the definitive, though hidden, revelation of God, *theologians of the cross do not reflect on God, the world, and humanity outside of the relationship that is revealed in the cross.*

This thesis expands upon the last. Luther claims that theologians of the cross will not fix their gaze upon God dwelling in majesty and power. Always true theologians are to know God graciously in relationship with humanity through Jesus Christ. Theologians of glory try to see the invisible properties of God as those properties are in and of themselves. But this quest to lift the veil and see God out of relation with humanity leads to the abandonment of mercy, both divine and human, in favor of

---

4. LW 31.33; WA 1.238.

5. Westhelle, *Voces de Protesta en América Latina*, 37–38 (trans. mine). Cf. Westhelle, "Communication and the Transgression of Language in Martin Luther," 7.

tyranny. Luther claimed that God outside of the christological relationship with humanity is a terrifying presence. Those who pursue such a God inevitably visit terror upon others.

In this way, the early Luther claimed that even God is most clearly defined at the strange extremity of divinity where God makes marginality a home upon the cross. God shares the place of those whom the world refuses to see. On the cross, the community of faith encounters God's self-defining act. Just as gazing at the luxurious beauty and power of Rome reveals less about the soundness of international systems than does looking at the suffering of Germany upon which Rome is built, so also looking only to God as imagined in power and pomp reveals less about God than the naked one hanging upon the cross. On the cross God hangs with humanity in its suffering. The preached, clothed, revealed God is always one who by unwavering, self-chosen commitment must be in relationship with humanity.

For this reason, theologians of the cross also will not reflect on what humans might be outside of their relationship with God. Their theology will not, for example, dwell on human beings seeking to do what is in themselves (*facere quod in se est*) apart from God. The insight regarding God's relational commitment was for Luther a direct attack on scholastic ideals. Rather theologians of the cross know only of God in relationship to humanity, with a priority given to the denseness of this relation in the midst of cross and suffering.

The relationality of this way of being a theologian includes not only the individual and God, but also the neighbor in need, the Marys, and thus the community as a whole. Luther begins to articulate this in the public indulgence controversy where he attacks the church that has sought an existence solely unto itself. This communal dimension is also clear in Luther's sermon on the sacrament where the body mentioned in the title is not in the first place the sacramental host, but the community gathered. God in Christ transubstantiates the community so that it truly becomes the body of Christ. And any who would wish to have Christ without their neighbor eat and drink to their own death. As with the sacramental elements, so Christ also is truly present through the community. Christ's act of transformation of that community gains a fragile but real foothold for God's transforming presence in history. The relationship is not merely external, but takes shape in the community of the cross. This community serves the world as a servant of Christ crucified rather than Christ glorified as Luther argued and the pamphlet literature illustrated. At times, in fact, not only is God's solidarity not limited to an individual relationship, it may even to the whole people, the German people in Luther's time, at the edges of economic, political, and religious power.

3. Since theologians of the cross live and think in a way that is centered in Christ crucified as the definitive, though hidden, revelation of God, *they will not flee from those realities of conflict that resemble the cross of Christ in their own day.* Thus Luther became a theologian of the cross in the concrete polemical context of conflict with one of the most powerful public institutions of his day. Remove the theology of the cross from the context of conflict and it loses its intensity.

Because of Luther's pastoral concern and his discontentment with the public practices of his own church, Luther's theology of the cross comes into being and gains a hearing. As stated at the end of the last thesis, the church was not only a religious organization but was hopelessly intertwined, and this in an oppressive way, with the political, economic, and social intrigues of its day. Thus the theology of the cross was theo-logico-*social* critique. Luther accused the church of being a church of glory buttressed by its servants, the theologians of glory. He accused the pope of serving as vicar of a glorified Christ, rather than the cruci-fied Christ. Those who should be feeding the sheep were fleecing them instead and in the process they are bleeding Germany dry. In this they were not alone. A partnership in this oppression developed between the Fuggers and the papacy. In this capacity, the Fuggers received as much profits from indulgence traffic as did St. Peter's. Luther's attacks upon the papacy and the Fuggers become utter condemnations.

Those attacks were finally translated in a clear and scathing man-ner when they moved into visual media in the pamphlets. In particular the visual representations of the *Passion of Christ and of the Antichrist* is virulent. The whole life of Christ was his passion, and not his death alone; his life was used to critique of the institutional church as led by the pope of Luther's day. That series of twenty-six drawings mounted an attack against the church's quest for power, prestige, pomp, and profits. Christ refused to be made king; the pope claimed worldly power in the fiction of the Donation of Constantine. Christ wore a crown of thorns; the pope sought a triple tiara. Christ lived with the sick and poor; the pope was honored by military processions. Jesus washed his disciples' feet; the pope demanded that his own be kissed. Jesus had no place to lay his head; the pope had amassed the estates of the Vatican. Jesus rode a donkey into Jerusalem; the pope rode a stallion of war. Jesus carried a cross; the pope was carried through towns and villages in pompous style. Jesus paid taxes; the pope bled Germany dry by extracting taxes. Finally, the pope was seen descending into hell, while Christ ascended into heaven. Throughout the images, the pope is surrounded by symbols of wealth, power—often surrounded by a glut of armed military personnel—and honor. Christ lived like the poor who gazed upon the pamphlet. In the visual representation of the theology of the cross, the poor saw the solidarity of Jesus with them in their daily struggles. Christ came out in solidarity for their sake.

In all his life practices, Jesus was a theologian of the cross. Those theologians who legitimized injustice were theologians of glory. They were guilty of *volatilem cognitatum*[6], knowledge prone to erupt in violence. Luther's understanding of the forms of this violence was broad as stated in the *Heidelberg Disputation* and further illustrated in the *Magnificat*. Social scorn and economic tyranny attacked fools like Luther and poor people like Mary. The persecuted Luther clearly understood this violent knowledge in light of his own experience at Worms. From the strongly antithetical style of the *Heidelberg Disputation* to the drawings of the *Passion of Christ*, the theology of the cross appears over and against that which would negate it.

One of the concepts that Luther used to attack the papacy and the scholastic theologians of glory who supported it was his notion of the bound or enslaved will. Luther's use of this concept functioned in a particular tactical way to dethrone the reigning theologians of his day. He attacked their particular pretensions: their self-aggrandizing claims and their faith in their own progress. Luther's definition of bondage was a fluid concept. He became concerned with much more concrete

6. WA 1.362.16–17; cf. LW 31.53.

166 CROSS IN TENSIONS

forms of social enslavements in those documents directed at the common people. In these he did not turn from spiritual enslavement, but expanded his definition of it to include poverty, social stratification, disdain, usury, taxation, and religious manipulation.

4. Since theologians of the cross live and think in a way that is centered in Christ crucified as the definitive, though hidden, revelation of God, *they recognize that the world is divided by specific life and death conflicts. They also recognize that the word of God will be heard differently according to one's location within these struggles.*

Luther's literature reflects this fact as the changes that accompany the choice of language of the documents illustrate. The differences between the concerns in Latin documents and those in German documents illustrate the change he made in the way he proclaimed the word as he addressed different communities. Those who spoke the official legal language of church and empire heard a more pointedly polemical word directed at them. Both the *Heidelberg Disputation* and the *Ninety-Five Theses* demonstrate the way that Luther was willing to launch an offensive against those who were privileged. In Luther's German works the common hearer found that Luther's attacks were launched not at them, but in their favor against a powerful enemy. In many of the devotional tracts directed to the common German people, Luther avoided polemic against his audience to speak a pure word of divine comfort to the afflicted.

Luther explicitly stated this dynamic commitment in the *Commentary on the Magnificat.* There he confessed that God is the "kind of Lord who accomplishes nothing else than only exalting those who are lowly, and lowering those who are exalted, in short, who breaks what is established and who establishes what is broken."[7] Mary in the *Magnificat* is not merely understood for her place in the church, but for her place in society. In fact, Luther understands the reason that God chose her to be her *unansehelich Wesen,* her lowly place in society. Furthermore Luther interpreted Mary in terms of one major disenfran-

---

7. Trans. mine, LW 21.299; WA 7.546.32–34.

chised group of his own day, domestic servants. He explicitly claims that God intentionally did not choose a queen's daughter as the means of incarnation, but a poor, despised servant. How odd and empowering it must have been for the many people who were serving as domestic servants to hear of Mary, God's chosen, described not as a queen, whether of heaven or earth, but in their own image!

Related to this is Luther's understanding of *creatio ex nihilo*. Luther interpreted the "nothing" not primarily as "non-existence," but in terms of the poor who are nothing, who do not even exist, in the eyes of the world. God always and everywhere creates out of nothing, out of the have-nothings (*Habennichts*). The division that concerned Luther in that commentary was not God versus universal humanity, but God and God's chosen poor versus the godless mighty ones. Luther warned of the power of the word that "constrains you to fear if you are mighty, and to take comfort if you are of low degree. And the mightier you are, the more you must fear; the lowlier you are, the more you must take comfort."[8]

This theme is clearly embodied in pamphlet literature where the common person was the one who understood the ways of God. They gazed at the saving, crucified Christ, while the powerful sought to place themselves over him or to turn their back from him and flee. Time and time again, the clear divisions that Luther declaimed were not about generic human potential in the face of God, but rather fell upon the fault lines of power in the society of his day. Luther's addressed the economic, political, ecclesiastical, and social antagonisms of his day.

5. Since theologians of the cross live and think in a way that is centered in Christ crucified as the definitive, though hidden, revelation of God, *they know that God defies the established order and finally turns the world upside-down when God turns the divine gaze toward the poor and suffering people.*

This theme is again most clear in the *Magnificat*. The basis of this revolution is God's gracious gaze. The *Ansehen* of God is focused on those of *unansehelich Wesen*. God respects the disrespected! And this changes

8. LW 21.306; WA 7.553.21–554.2.

everything. The totally alternative vision of God is offered. This is true in a double sense. It is first an alternative vision looking at God hanging on the cross; God is the one we see in this hidden way. But also it is a vision *from* the same God who is initiating a new way of seeing all else. To hold to Christ is to have a completely new world.

The basis of this new vision is the crucified Christ. The new reality becomes real for the people in the word and in the celebration of the Lord's Supper. There Christ enters into solidarity with those who suffer. He makes their sufferings his own. Again we recall how radical and complete this solidarity actually is. Their sufferings *are* Christ's; his help and name *are* theirs!

The pamphlet on the passion of Christ also illustrated the radically new way of living in the world that this perspective offers. The viewer stands at a crossroad and must choose between two alternative ways of living in the world.

In terms of Luther's Latin reading audience, Luther undercuts their old way of organizing the world when he rejected the law, even good law, as the dominant means through which God relates to people. Luther attacked the law and understood that it was not simply a spiritual dynamic related to the conscience of the individual, but was the very foundation for jurisprudence in all realms of life. Within both church and empire, the law functioned as the ground for all efforts at understanding, discerning, judging, and legislating. The one-time law student Luther invited theologians to abandon their penchant for a legal understanding of reality. He dismantled the basis for the old epistemology and then articulated this whole new world.

6. Since theologians of the cross live and think in a way that is centered in Christ crucified as the definitive, though hidden, revelation of God, *a totally new liberative vision of reality comes to light. Faith takes hold of this new world and lives in it.*

"To the extent that you believe it, you already have it," Luther was fond of saying. Faith teaches us to see in the dark where there is nothing to be seen. For the law says, "Do this!" and nothing is done; faith says,

"Believe this!" and everything is already done.[9] As Luther stated in the *Magnificat*, faith is the trust by which we are "suspended in God's love" or "caught up" in the new reality.[10] *Vivimus in abscondito Dei*, claimed Luther in *Heidelberg Disputation*. "We live in the hiddenness of God."[11] And what Luther means by this is "in naked trust in God's mercy." It is this naked faith, clinging to Christ and living in the transformed world (*Verkehrte Welt*) which Christ offers that grants the experience of new life. The theology of the cross is always a theology of faith.

This reversal or transformation has consequences for the life of the faithful. Again, we recall the strong reversal of what is truly godly living as it was presented in the *Passion of Christ*. God calls on the faithful to notice how God is present in lowliness rather than pomp and power. God calls Mary and her people to trust the gracious regard of God when all around them says they are nothing. Faith offers a strange new world in which Mary gladly takes up residency in spite of all the voices around her that would bring her down.

Faith also plays an essential role in epistemology. Luther's early theology of the cross depends on faith to hold it together. He has attacked the reigning intellectual systems of the day in part because all the pieces of their reflections fit together too well. Luther's early articulations have a thoughtfully reflective, *ad hoc* quality to them. This is not merely due to the fact that he was a biblical scholar rather than a systematic theologian. It was because he was a theologian of the cross who knew that closed systems close out the newness that God brings. Such theologies of glory have a predictable tendency to exclude from their purview the very people God has chosen. They can speak so unambiguously because they have shut their eyes to troublesome and disturbing aspects of reality.

In his early years, Luther does not dismantle one intellectual system to replace it with another, though he does find himself drawn in that direction as the years pass. Thus the systematizing of his own thought was not immune to the temptation to eliminate the troublesome and disturbing aspects of his world. But in his early thought, coherence was found in trusting the God who was hidden in the cross; the

---

9. LW 31.41; WA 1.354.31–32.

10. LW 21.307; WA 7.554.21–22.

11. Trans. mine, cf. LW 31.44; WA 1.357.3

crucified God was, and even had to be, enough. As Westhelle observes with Luther, in the strange crucified presence of God a broken and fragmented reality is made visible. "Wholeness is won by a faith that sees in the dispersed fragments of the world the reintegrative and marvelous force of divine grace."[12] The cross of Christ that shatters all pretensions to perfection, including both the sinful claim to know everything perfectly and all projects of triumphal progress, is the same cross that holds the world and the future together through the act of faith. The one who shatters what is established is the same who makes whole what has been broken. And we too can live in such a world not by a self-confident act of putting it all back together in our minds, but through trusting the one who promises final wholeness. Trust or faith in God distrusts flawless human explanatory systems. The new world is not received by the mind's clear sight, but by the heart's faithful trust.

7. Since theologians of the cross live and think in a way that is centered in Christ crucified as the definitive, though hidden, revelation of God, *they bear witness to that gracious, broken presence in the way that they practice their own vocation in service to the suffering people.*

Finally, in these theses we have talked of theologians of the cross more than of the theology of the cross. This is no accident. The process we have described demands the total life of the faithful. The final test of theologians of the cross is if they are conformed to God's vision and serve the disrespected ones. In theses 19 and 20 of the *Heidelberg Disputation*, Luther wrote, "That person is not worthy to be called 'theologian' who sees the invisible properties of God, comprehended in glory and majesty. Rather that person [is worthy to be called 'theologian'] who comprehends the visible properties and backside of God, seen in suffering and the cross."[13] Käseman was faithful to Luther when he wrote, "doctrinal claims without suffering discipleship is bloodless and vague."[14] The theology of the cross is about a way of thinking and

12. Westhelle and Götz, "In Quest of a Myth," 20.
13. Trans. mine, cf. LW 31.40; WA 1.354.17–20.
14. Käsemann, *Jesus Means Freedom*, 149.

living in the world at service to the God who is servant to the poor. Theologians of the cross are faithful when they interpret the cross in the tensions of the world in service of the poor; when theologians abuse the cross by forcing it to serve the status quo against the needs of the poor, they are at odds with divine intentions revealed in the cross of Christ. They use the cross against itself causing cross intentions.

In this sense the theme of this book is as much about how we live as believers as it is about the specific doctrine in which we believe. For Luther, the Christian was to be *fureinander*,[15] for the neighbor in need in one's vocation whatever that might be. Among Luther's own vocations was that of "doctor of theology." This means that being a theologian of the cross meant serving the neighbor in need as Luther did his work of theology. "It is not sufficient, and it does no one any good, to know God in glory and majesty, unless that one know the same in the lowliness and shame of the cross."[16] Remember Luther's double point in that thesis. Do not think of God as God is in glory and majesty, but as God is in lowliness and shame. But also, do not let your place of interpretation be in glory and majesty, but in lowliness and shame, in solidarity with Mary and her people. This has not always been the history of the cross; the earth is crying out with the blood of the victims killed by those who bore the image of the cross on their standards. The theologian of the cross in action must be the reverse of the theologian of glory, preferring sufferings to works, cross to glory, the weak to the powerful, the fools to the wise, and universally that which is taken by the world as evil over that which the world lauds and pursues as good.

Though at his worst Luther lapsed from this practice, when at his best he knew this to be the case. He wrote in 1519:

> Thus my learning is not my own; it belongs to the unlearned and is the debt I owe to them. . . . Thus my wisdom belongs to the foolish, my power to the oppressed. Thus my wealth belongs to the poor, my righteousness to the sinners.[17]

This principle is helpful to us as we seek to discern when Luther faithfully followed the crucified in solidarity with the poor and when he strayed from this call. Rather than proclaim that Luther was con-

15. LW 35.52; WA 2.743.40.
16. Trans. mine, cf. LW 31.52–53; WA 1.362.11–13.
17. LW 27.393; WA 2.606.4–10.

sistently a theologian of the cross, we must ask whose interests were served in each moment that he addressed. We have argued that he was most clearly serving the cross and its poor in his early years. Later his own quest to establish his movement as well as the progressive systematizing of his own thought led to a betrayal of the clarity of this commitment. This principle still is essential to us as we ourselves strive to be theologians of the cross in this new day. So let us sing with Mary![18]

18. LW 21.306; WA 7.553.21.

The Passion of the Christ and of the Antichrist[1]

Translated by Keith Killinger

1. The full German text is available at http://www.pitts.emory.edu/dia/complete_
works.cfm. All biblical citations in the original included only chapter references. In the
translation, verses have been added to clarify the citation.

of Christ

When Jesus realized that they were going to come and make him king, he fled instead up the mountain, alone (John 6:15). My kingdom is not of this world (John 18:36). The world's kings rule, and those who have power are called "gracious lords," but not so with you; rather whoever is greater among you shall lower himself to the least (Luke 22:25f).

# of 𝔄𝔫𝔱𝔦𝔠𝔥𝔯𝔦𝔰𝔱

𝔒n the basis of the unquestionable supremacy which we have over the empire, and by our authority, we have a legitimate claim to the imperial succession, should it become vacant. (clem. pastoralis ad fi. de sen. et re judi.) *Summa Summarum:*[2] 𝔑othing else in the 'Spiritual Law' of the Pope is as clear as its elevation of this idol and antichrist above all emperors, kings and princes, as Peter foretold: "There will come impudent bishops who despise the earthly authorities" (2 Peter 2:1,10).

2. This Latin phrase can either refer to "the highest height" or the "final summary." In this case the two come together since the final summary of their theology is a critique of their infatuation with ruling on high. "Crowning point" might capture both senses well.

of Christ

The soldiers wove a crown of thorns and pressed it on his head, then garbed him in a purple robe. (John 19:2)

# of Antichrist

The emperor Constantine has handed over the imperial crown, ornaments and other finery appropriate for the emperor to wear, purple robes, and all the other robes and scepters, for us to bear and use. (c. Constantius xcvi dis.) In order to preserve their tyranny they have put forth lies like this, which contradict all history and custom, for it was not the usual manner of the Roman Caesars to wear such a crown.

# of Christ

As I have washed your feet—I, who am your lord and master—
much more should you, among yourselves, wash each others' feet.
Here I have given you a sign and example: as I have done to you,
you should do the same from now on. Truly, truly I say to you, the
servant is not greater than his master, nor is the dispatched messenger greater than the one who sent him. Are you aware of this?
Blessed be you, if you will do it. (John 13:14–17)

# of Antichrist

The Pope is so presumptuous as to mimic certain rulers and hea-
then princes who extend their feet so that people may kiss them, so
that what was written might come true: "Whoever does not worship
the image of this beast is to be killed" (Apocalypse 13:15). In his
decretals, the Pope shamelessly takes pride in such kissing. (c.
cum olin de pri. cle. Si summos pon. de sen. excom.)

of Christ

Go to the sea and put in your hook; open the mouth of the first fish that takes it; therein you will find a gulden. Give it as the tax for me and you. (Matthew 17:27) To the authority who bears the sword in its hands, give what it is due: the tax to whom taxes are due, the toll to whom it is due. (Paul to the Romans, 13:4, 6, 7)

# of Antichrist

Under penalty of severe ban and interdict, we establish and ordain
that it is improper for those who have worldly jurisdiction to impose taxes and tribute on the spiritual estate or to demand the same
of its houses or goods. Likewise, the spiritual estate should not
pay any of these without our permission. (c. i. de immunit. eccle.
li. vi.) Thus the Pope has torn apart God's command with his
own—of which his unChristian decretal is a singular example.

of Christ

Though he was in the divine form, yet Christ divested himself of it, lowered himself, and behaved as a servant, appearing like other men; and being found a man, he humbled himself. And he was obedient unto death. (To the Philippians 2:6–8)

of Antichrist

The Pope deems that it would be detrimental to his honor were he to act humbly, for contempt grows against the authority of one who humbles himself too much. (c. quando 86. distinc.) Hence the gloss: "This is true with fools." That is to say, "It is necessary to govern the German fools harshly so that they think we are important."

of Christ

Since Jesus had journeyed a long distance, he was tired (John 4:6). The one who wants to follow me must take up his cross upon himself and come after me (Matthew 16:24). He carried his own cross and went to the place which is called Calvary (John 19:17).

# of Antichrist

The chapter Si quis suadente and others like it show quite well
how willing the Pope is to bear the cross of offense: he damns and
hands over to the devil any who lay a hand on the priests.
And this too is how the Pope "bears" the cross: that baptized
Christians have to carry *him* on their shoulders!

of Christ

I must also preach the kingdom of God in other cities, for I was
sent for this purpose and have preached in synagogues throughout
Galilee. (Luke 4:43, 44)

# of Antichrist

It often happens that bishops are overwhelmed by many tasks and at times, because of involvement in warfare, cannot even perform them at all, which should not be. So that preaching may not be hindered, especially when their sees are large, they may appoint others in their stead who shall preach. (c. Inter cetera de offi. ordina.) There are bishops who forget their ordained office and become animalia ventris[3] and say, "Come, let's feast and make merry, and enjoy the good life forever!" (Isaiah 56:12)

3. This Latin phrase means "beasts or animals [ruled by their] stomachs."

of Christ

Foxes have their holes and birds of the air their nests, but the Son of Man has nothing on which he might lay his head (Luke 9:58). This one, although he was rich, nevertheless for our sakes became poor, and his poverty has made us rich (2 Corinthians 8:9).

# of Antichrist

We undo all oaths which the spiritual estate have given under duress and command that one must protect their property, not only with the "spiritual," but also with the physical, sword until such time as they reclaim the assets wrested from them. (15. q. 6. c. Auctoritatem.) And whoever dies or is ruined in this war shall attain eternal life. (23. q. 5. c. omnium. Et q. 8. c. omni.) This is to be so conscious of one's goods that he looks to them for benefit, even though Christ's blood was poured out for him.

of Christ

Look! Your king comes to you humble, on a young donkey
(Matthew 21:5). Thus has Christ come, riding on a stranger's
donkey, poor and meek, and rides not to impose his rule but to give
us all his blessed death (John 12:15).

# of Antichrist

The spiritual estate are all kings—as evidenced by the 'tonsure-crowns' on their heads. (duo 12 q. i.) The Pope may ride just as the emperor does, and the emperor is his footman, in order that the standards of episcopal dignity might not be diminished. (c. constantinus 96. dis.) The Pope is set above all peoples and kingdoms. (Extravag. Super gentes, Iohannis 22.)

of Christ

You shall possess neither gold nor silver, nor money in your belt; no purse, neither two cloaks nor extra shoes, nor walking staff (Matthew 10:9–10). St Peter says, "I have neither gold nor silver" (Acts 3:6). Where then is "Peter's Patrimony?"

# of Antichrist

No bishop shall be consecrated in an unimportant or small town. Rather, he shall be granted an honorable title and highly esteemed. (80. dist c. Episcopi.) We command that no consecration shall be valid without ample provision of a living. (70. dist. Sanctorum.)

of Christ

The kingdom of God is not in external manifestation: "Behold, here—or there—is Christ!" but the kingdom of God is within you (Luke 17:20, 21). Why have you overturned the commandment of God for the sake of human law? All honor me futilely who hold to human teachings and commands (Matthew 15:3, 9; Isaiah 29:13).

# of Antichrist

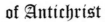

The dominion of the Antichrist consists entirely in external organization. What attests to the Pope's legitimacy apart from a system of chasubles, vestments, tonsures, holy days, consecrations, benefices, orders, monks and priests? Also their property and goods they call "spiritual" goods, themselves alone "the Christian church," and the priests "the chosen people of God"—just as if the laity were not the Church nor of God, contrary to all of scripture. On top of that, he forbids eating and marriage, just as Paul had foretold: "then shall come lying spirits and such things shall be forbidden." (1 Timothy 4:1–3)

of Christ

He found vendors, sheep, oxen and doves, and money-changers sitting in the temple, and immediately made a whip of cords, drove all the sheep, oxen, doves and money-changers out of the temple, spilled the money, overturned the cash-boxes, and said to those who sold doves, "Get out of here with these! You shall not make a market of my Father's House!" (John 2:14–16). You received it free of charge, therefore give it free of charge (Matthew 10:8). May your money go with you into damnation! (Acts 8:20).

of Antichrist

Here sits the Antichrist in the temple of God and manifests himself as God, as Paul announces (2 Thessalonians 2:4), changes every divine ordinance, as Daniel says, and suppresses the holy scriptures, sells dispensations, indulgences, palliums, bishoprics, fiefs; gathers the treasures of the earth, annuls marriage, afflicts consciences with his laws, grants privileges and—where money is involved—tears them up; beatifies saints, blesses and curses unto the fourth generation, and orders that his voice be heeded as like unto God's own. (c. sic omnis. dis. 19.) And no one may argue with him. (17. q. 4. c. nemini.)

of Christ

As they watched, he was lifted up and the clouds took him from their sight. This Jesus who has been taken up from you into heaven will thus return, as you have seen him go into heaven (Acts 1:9, 11). His kingdom has no end (Luke 1:33). Whoever serves me, that one will follow me, and where I am, there my servant will be also (John 12:26).

# of Antichrist

The beast was seized, along with the false prophet who had done signs through him, with which he had misled those who had received his mark from him and worshipped his image. They were sunk in the lake of fire and sulfur, and slain by the sword that proceeded from the mouth of him who rode upon the white horse (Apocalypse 19:20, 21). Then shall the Rogue be revealed: him whom the Lord Jesus Christ shall slay by the breath of his mouth and will cast him down by the glory of his coming (2 Thessalonians 2:8).

Since something may not be labeled a 'Scandalous Book' or 'defamatory publication' unless it actually contains shameful calumny or criminality, it is clear that this booklet may not be deemed a 'Scandalous Book,' nor be forbidden under the laws which have been issued against libelous writings, because everything in it is to be found in the papal, spiritual laws as not only that which is proper, but legal as well. And it has been published in brief and summary form, in complete accord with the laws, both secular and spiritual, for the common good and the advancement of Christianity. Therefore take heed: there is even 'better' yet to come!

Bibliography

Althaus, Paul. "Die Bedeutung des Kreuzes im Denken Luthers." *Vierteljahrsschrift der Luthergesellschaft* 4 (1926) 97–107.

———. *The Theology of Martin Luther.* Translated by Robert C. Schultz. Philadelphia: Fortress, 1966.

Baeumer, Max L. "Was Luther's Reformation a Revolution?" In *The Martin Luther Quincentennial*, edited by Gerhard Dünnhaupt, 253–69. Detroit: Wayne State University Press, 1985.

Bakhtin, Mikhail. *Rabelais and His World.* Cambridge, MA: MIT Press, 1968.

Blickle, Peter. *Communal Reformation: The Quest for Salvation in Sixteenth-Century Germany.* Atlantic Highlands, NJ: Humanities, 1992.

———. *The Revolution of 1525: The German Peasants' War from a New Perspective.* Baltimore: John Hopkins University Press, 1981.

———. "Social Protest and Reformation Theology." In *Religion, Politics and Social Protest: Three Studies on Early Modern Germany*, edited by Kasper von Greyerz, 123. Boston: Allen & Unwin, 1984.

Böckmann, Paul. "Der gemeine Mann in den Flugschriften der Reformation." *Deutsche Vierteljahreschrift für Literaturwissenschaft und Geistesgeschichte* 22 (1944) 186–230.

Brady, Thomas, Jr. "Economic and Social Institutions." In *Germany: A New Social and Economic History.* Vol. 1 *(1450–1650)*, edited by Robert Scribner, 259–90. London: Arnold, 1996.

———. "Social History." In *Reformation Europe: A Guide to Research*, edited by Steven Ozment, 161–82. St. Louis: Center for Reformation Research, 1982.

Brecht, Martin. *Martin Luther.* Vol. 1, *His Road to Reformation, 1483–1521.* Philadelphia: Fortress, 1985.

Brendler, Gerhard. *Martin Luther: Theology and Revolution.* New York: Oxford, 1991.

Cole, Richard. "The Dynamics of Printing in the Sixteenth Century." In *The Social History of the Reformation*, edited by Lawrence P. Buck and Jonathon W. Zophy, 93–105. Columbus: Ohio State University Press, 1972.

Cochlaeus, Johannes. *Historia Martin Lutheri.* Translated by C. Hueber. Ingolstadt: Sartorium, 1582.

Dussel, Enrique. *The Invention of the Americas: Eclipse of "the Other" and the Myth of Modernity.* New York: Continuum, 1995.

Ebeling, Gerhard. "Die Definition des Menschen und seine Mortalität." In *Disputatio de Homine*, edited by Gerhard Ebeling, 60–102. Lutherstudien 2. Tübingen: Mohr Siebeck, 1982.

———. *Luther: An Introduction to His Thought.* Translated by R. A. Wilson. London: Collins, 1970.

Edwards, Mark U. Jr. *Printing, Propaganda, and Martin Luther.* Los Angeles: University of California Press, 1994.

Erasmus, Desiderius. *Discourse on Free Will.* Translated and edited by Ernst F. Winter. New York: Continuum, 2005.

Feuerbach, Ludwig. *The Essence of Faith according to Luther.* Translated by Melvin Cherno. New York: Harper & Row, [1967].

Forde, Gerhardt O. *On Being a Theologian of the Cross: Reflections on Luther's Heidelberg Disputation, 1518.* Grand Rapids: Eerdmans, 1997.

———. *Theology is for Proclamation.* Minneapolis: Fortress, 1990.

Friedrichs, Christopher R. "German Social Structure, 1300–1600." In *Germany: A New Social and Economic History.* Vol. 1, *1450–1650,* edited by Bob Scribner, 233–58. London: Arnold, 1996.

Grane, Leif. *The Augsburg Confession: A Commentary.* Minneapolis: Augsburg, 1987.

Grimm, Harold J. *The Reformation Era, 1500–1650.* 2nd ed. New York: Macmillan, 1973.

Hall, Douglas John. *God and human Suffering: An Exercise in the Theology of the Cross.* Minneapolis: Augsburg, 1986.

———. *Thinking the Faith: Christian Theology in a North American Context.* Minneapolis: Augsburg, 1988.

———. *Lighten Our Darkness: Toward an Indigenous Theology of the Cross.* Rev. ed. Lima, OH: Academic Renewal, 2001.

———. *The Cross in Our Context: Jesus and the Suffering World.* Minneapolis: Fortress, 2003.

Hillerbrand, Hans J. "The German Reformation and the Peasants' War." In *The Social History of the Reformation,* edited by Lawrence P. Buck and Jonathon W. Zophy, 106–37. Columbus: Ohio State University Press, 1972.

Hillerbrand, Hans J., ed. *The Reformation: A Narrative History Related by Contemporary Observers and Participants.* New York: Harper & Row, 1964.

Käsemann, Ernst. *Jesus Means Freedom.* Translated by Frank Clarke. Philadelphia: Fortress, 1969.

Lindberg, Carter. *The European Reformations.* Cambridge, MA: Blackwell, 1996.

Loewenich, Walther von. *Luther's Theology of the Cross.* Translated by Herbert J. A. Bouman. Minneapolis: Augsburg, 1976.

Lohse, Bernhard. *Martin Luther: An Introduction to His Life and Work.* Translated by Robert C. Schultz. Philadelphia: Fortress, 1986.

Madsen, Anna M. *The Theology of the Cross in Historical Perspective.* Distinguished Dissertations in Christian Theology. Eugene, OR: Pickwick, 2007.

McGrath, Alister. *Luther's Theology of the Cross: Martin Luther's Theological Breakthrough.* Cambridge, MA: Blackwell, 1985.

Moeller, Bernd. *Imperial Cities and the Reformation: Three Essays.* Edited and Translated by H. C. Erick Midelfort and Mark U. Edwards Jr. Philadelphia: Fortress, 1972.

Nelson, Benjamin. *The Idea of Usury from Tribal Brotherhood to Universal Otherhood.* 2nd ed. Chicago: University of Chicago Press, 1969.

Oberman, Heiko A. *Luther: Man between God and the Devil.* Translated by Eileen Walliser-Schwarzbart. New York: Doubleday, 1992.

———. "The Gospel of Social Unrest." In *The German Peasant War of 1525: New Viewpoints*, edited by Robert Scribner and Gerhard Benecke, 39–51. London: Allen & Unwin, 1979.

Ozment, Steven. *Protestants: The Birth of a Revolution*. New York: Doubleday, 1992.

Pfister, Christian. "The Population of Late Medieval and Early Modern Germany." In *Germany: A New Social and Economic History*. Vol. 1 *(1450–1650)*, edited by Robert Scribner, 33–62. London: Arnold, 1996.

Prenter, Regin. "Luther's Theology of the Cross." In *Publications of the Lutheran World Federation* 6 (Lutheran World Federation: Geneva, 1959–1960) 222–33.

Peura, Simo. *Mehr als ein Mensch?: Die Vergöttlichung als Thema der Theologie Martin Luthers von 1513 bis 1519*. Mainz: Zabern, 1994.

Rice, Eugene, with Anthony Grafton. *The Foundations of Early Modern Europe, 1460–1559*. New York: Norton, 1994.

Rösener, Werner. "The Agrarian Economy, 1300–1600." In *Germany: A New Social and Economic History*. Vol. 1, *1450–1650*, edited by Robert Scribner, 63–84. London: Arnold, 1996.

Ruge–Jones, Philip. *The Word of the Cross in a World of Glory*. Minneapolis: Fortress, 2008.

Russell, Paul. *Lay Theology in the Reformation: Popular Pamphleteers in Southwest Germany: 1521–1525*. Cambridge: Cambridge University Press, 1985.

Schöffler, Herbert. *Die Reformation: Einführung in eine Geistesgeschiche der deutschen Neuzeit*. Bochum-Langendreer: Pöppinghaus, 1936.

Scott, Tom. "Economic Landscapes." In *Germany: A New Social and Economic History*. Vol. 1, *1450–1650*, edited by Robert Scribner, 1–32. London: Arnold, 1996.

Scott, Tom, and Robert Scribner, editors. *The German Peasants' War: A History in Documents*. Atlantic Highlands, NJ: Humanities, 1991.

Scribner, Robert. *For the Sake of Simple Folk: Popular Propaganda for the German Reformation*. Cambridge: Harvard University Press, 1981.

———. *The German Reformation*. Atlantic Highlands, NJ: Humanities, 1986.

———. "Germany." In *The Reformation in National Context*, edited by Robert Scribner et al., 4–29. Cambridge: Harvard University Press, 1994.

———. "Oral Culture and the Transmission of Reformation Ideas." In *The Transmission of Ideas in the Lutheran Reformation*, edited by Helga Robinson-Hammerstein, 83–104. Worcester, England: Irish Academic, 1989.

———. *Popular Culture and Popular Movements in Reformation Germany*. London: Hambledon, 1987.

———. "Reformation, Carnival, and the World Turned Upside-down." *Social History* 3 (1977) 303–29.

Solberg, Mary. *Compelling Knowledge: A Feminist Proposal for an Epistemology of the Cross*. New York: State University of New York Press, 1997.

Spitz, Lewis. "Luther's Social Concern for Students." In *The Social History of the Reformation*, edited by Lawrence P. Buck and Jonathon W. Zophy, 249–71. Columbus: Ohio State University Press, 1972.

Steven-Arroyo, Anthony M., and Ana María Díaz-Stevens, editors. *An Enduring Flame: Studies on Latino Popular Religiosity*. New York: Bildner Center for Western Hemisphere Studies, 1994.

Vercruysse, Jos. "Luther's Theology of the Cross at the time of *Heidelberg Disputation.*" *Gregorianum* 57 (1976) 523–48.

———. "Luther's Theology of the Cross: Its Relevance for Ecumenism." *Centro Pro Unione* 35 (Spring 1989) 2–11.

Westhelle, Vítor. "Communication and the Transgression of Language in Luther." *Lutheran Quarterly* 17 (2003) 1–27.

———, with Hanna Betina Götz. "In Quest of a Myth: Latin American Literature and Theology." *Journal of Hispanic/Latino Theology* 3, (August 1995) 5–22.

———. Luther and Liberation." *Dialog* 25 (1986) 51–58.

———. *The Scandalous God: The Use and Abuse of the Cross.* Minneapolis: Fortress, 2007.

———. *Voces de Protesta en América Latina.* Mexico: CETPJDR/LSTC, 2000.

Wiesner, Merry E. "Gender and the Worlds of Work." In *Germany: A New Social and Economic History.* Vol. 1, *1450–1650,* edited by Robert Scribner, 209–32. London: Arnold, 1996.

Wright, William. "The Nature of Early Capitalism." In *Germany: A New Social and Economic History.* Vol. 1, *1450–1650,* edited by Robert Scribner, 181–208. London: Arnold, 1996.